Typhon Two heads are better than one.
But one hundred and one heads are
better than two!

Typhon
Let's face it. I was born first. I should rule heaven and earth!

Zeus
Ex*cuse* me?!?

The Graces
Oh, no, please excuse *us*!

Cyclopes
Say, can we interest you ladies in some bling?

Echo
BLING! BLING! BLING! BLING! BLING!
BLING! BLING! BLING! BLING! BLING!

Medusa
Hey, Echo! Look at me!

Minotaur invites everyone for dinner in his maze. No strings attached!

 Demeter
I'll bring cereal!

 Theseus
I'll bring teenagers!

 Eos
Oooohhh, I just *love* teenagers.

 Eros
Love? Did somebody call me?

 Sirens
La, la, la. Fly over here, you little cutie.

CONTENT CONSULTANT
William Hansen
Professor Emeritus of Classical Studies and Folklore
Indiana University, Bloomington

Library of Congress Cataloging-in-Publication Data
Kelly, Sophia.
What a beast! : a look-it-up guide to the monsters and mutants of
mythology! / Sophia Kelly.
p. cm. -- (Mythlopedia)
Includes bibliographical references and index.
ISBN-13: 978-1-60631-028-1 (lib. bdg.) 978-1-60631-060-1 (pbk.)
ISBN-10: 1-60631-028-3 (lib. bdg.) 1-60631-060-7 (pbk.)
1. Monsters--Encyclopedias, Juvenile. 2. Mythology,
Greek--Encyclopedias, Juvenile. I. Title.
BL795.M65K46 2009
398'.4093803--dc22

All rights reserved. Published by Franklin Watts, an imprint of Scholastic Inc.
Published simultaneously in Canada. Printed in China.
SCHOLASTIC, FRANKLIN WATTS, and associated logos are
trademarks and/or registered trademarks of Scholastic Inc.
4 5 6 7 8 9 10 R 18 17 16 15 14 13 12   62

MYTHLOPEDIA
WHAT A
BEAST!

I'm really just a cuddly kitty!

A Look-It-Up Guide to the Monsters and Mutants of Mythology

SOPHIA KELLY

■SCHOLASTIC

WHAT A BEAST!

HOT SPOTS OF
ANCIENT GREECE 4

TMI 10

PROFILES AND MYTHS

Up close and personal with the monsters and mutants of Greek mythology

THE AMAZONS 16
Hippolyte's Belt • The Abduction of Antiope • Penthesileia
and Achilles

BALIUS AND XANTHUS 20
Gift Horses • Fresh Horses

THE CENTAURS 24
A Cloudy Start • Wedding Crashers • Chiron: A Different Kind of Centaur •
The Death of Chiron • The Death of Heracles

CERBERUS 30
The Capture of Cerberus • Rock-a-Bye Puppy

THE CHIMERA 34
Trouble in the Neighborhood • Chimera Gets the Last Laugh

THE CYCLOPES 38
What a Family! • Making the Goods for the Gods • Death of the
Cyclopes • Happy with Hephaestus • A Hero Drops By •
A Dramatic Escape • *Eye Candy*

I see you!

Medusa

THE GIGANTES 46
The Birth of the Gigantes • Gigantes vs. Olympians: Round One • Gigantes vs. Olympians: Round Two • Gigantes vs. Olympians: The Final Round

THE HARPIES 50
Harping on Phineus • Stormy Meets Calm • Kill the Messengers

THE HECATONCHEIRES 54
Father of the Year—Not! • Horrifying Help

HYDRA 58
Hydra's Family Album • Hydra and Heracles • Hydra Kills

MEDUSA 62
Medusa and Athena • Medusa and Perseus • Medusa's Dead Head • The Graeae • Gorgons and Graeae and More, Oh My • *Medusa Makeover*

THE MINOTAUR 70
The Birth of the Minotaur • Fast Food • In the Labyrinth • Theseus and Ariadne • Daedalus and Icarus

PEGASUS 76
Inspiration of the Muses • Pegasus and Bellerophon • Winged Heroes

PROPHETS AND ORACLES 80
Calchas Sees the Way to Victory • Phineus and the Harpies • The Oracle at Delphi • Tiresias Loses His Sight • *Wheel of Misfortune*

PYTHON 86
Python Meets Apollo • Python Rots • Fun and Games

THE SATYRS 90
Silenus and King Midas • Musical Throwdown

THE SIRENS 94
The Sirens and Odysseus • The Sirens and the Argonauts

THE SPHINX 98
The Riddle of the Sphinx • The Story of Oedipus • Oedipus: From Bad to Worse • ... And Worse • *Welcome to Ms. Sphinx's Class*

TRITON 104
Triton and the Argonauts • Triton's Temper • Triton's Tritons

TYPHON 108
The Birth of Typhon • Typhon vs. Zeus • Love Is Blind

FAMILY PORTRAIT 112
FAMILY TREE 114
GLOSSARY 116
STARS OF GREEK MYTHOLOGY 118
FURTHER READING ... 120
WEB SITES 121
INDEX 122
CREDITS 127

You rock, Mom!

Pegasus

THE MYTHLOPEDIA INTRODUCTION

Are you ready to get your myth on? Then you've come to the right place: MYTHLOPEDIA, your one-stop shop for everything you need to know about the stars of Greek mythology. From gods and monsters to goddesses and heroes, the myths that rocked the ancient world are ready to rock yours—if you're ready to read on! But first, check out a little background info that will help you make sense of these amazing characters and stories.

So, what is mythology?

Good question! "Mythology" is the word used to describe *all* the myths of a particular society. People who specialize in studying myths are called "mythologists." From the Yoruba of West Africa to the Inca of South America, from the Norse of Europe to the Navajo of North America, every culture has its own myths that help us understand its customs and ways of viewing the world.

What is a myth?

Simply put, a myth is a kind of story. But not just any old story! Most myths have one or more of these characteristics:

➤ Myths are usually about gods, goddesses, or supernatural beings with greater powers and abilities than ordinary humans.

➤ Myths explain the origins of the world or how human customs came to be.

➤ Myths take place in a time long, long ago, usually in the earliest days of humanity (or just before humans showed up on Earth).

➤ Myths were usually thought to be true by their original tellers—no matter how wild or strange they seem to us.

TWO NAMES, POWERS THE SAME

Many gods and goddesses have both Greek and Roman names. That's because the ancient Romans adopted a great deal of Greek mythology and made it their own. Generally, that deity's powers and myths stayed the same— even though he or she had a new name. As a result, the study of Greek and Roman mythology is often grouped together under the name "classical mythology."

What is the purpose of myths?

A better question might be, What *isn't* the purpose of myths? Myths can:

➤ explain how things came to be—like the origin of the universe or the creation of humans;

➤ teach people about the values and beliefs that are important in their society; and

➤ contain deep religious significance to the people who tell and believe in them.

Perhaps most importantly, studying myths can teach us about people around the world—their cultures and what is (or was) important to them.

Do myths really matter today? After all, mortals have reality TV.

Absolutely! References to Greek mythology are all around us.

➤ Ever heard of Nike brand athletic gear? Meet Nike, personification and goddess of victory.

➤ What would Valentine's Day be without the god of love, Cupid—or Eros, as the ancient Greeks called him?

➤ Does *Apollo 13* ring a bell? The first crewed U.S. space missions were named for Apollo, the god of archery and prophecy.

Bottom line: References to ancient myths are everywhere, from science to pop culture, and knowing about them will help you understand more about the world we live in.

HOW DID WE LEARN THESE STORIES?

At first, Greek mythology was passed along orally through storytelling, songs, and poetry. We learned the stories from written versions, such as Homer's epic poems *The Iliad* and *The Odyssey*, which tell about the great deeds of heroes. Other sources are Hesiod's *Theogony*, which describes the origins of the world and the gods, and the *Homeric Hymns*, a collection of poems addressed to different gods.

WAB

WHAT A BEAST

What was a typical day like for a monster of Greek mythology?
In a word: beastly! We don't want to point fingers, but a three-headed pooch fell asleep on the job; a hideous serpent terrorized the neighborhood and lost her head, er, heads; and an ugly Gorgon turned her enemies to stone with a glance. Sound like your worst nightmare? Well, it's all true—or is it?

In ancient stories, beastly creatures served an important purpose. They represented evil in conflicts between good and bad (and gave mortals the chance to slay them and become heroes). In the days before science offered so many answers, the monsters of myth provided explanations for disasters such as shipwrecks (sea nymphs lured sailors to destruction with their singing) and volcanoes (fire-breathing creatures lived under mountains, of course!).

We could go on and on, but the beasts can say (or growl) it so much better themselves. So get ready, mortals. You're about to get up close and personal with some of the wildest, weirdest, and most wicked creatures of Greek mythology!

 **Typhon** Monsters rule!

Profile of The Amazons

Sounds Like: am'-uh-zonz

Generation:
- ☐ Titan
- ☐ Olympian
- ☑ Other: Female warriors

Special Abilities: Archery
Fighting

Characteristics: Courage
Strength

Attributes: Arrows
Bows
Shields

Top 10 Things to Know About Us:

10. Our favorite deities are Artemis, goddess of hunting, and Ares, god of war.

9. We raise only our daughters—don't even ask about our sons.

8. Achilles killed our queen, Penthesileia, during the Trojan War.

7. Theseus abducted our sister Antiope, so we followed him to Athens.

6. Give us a bow and arrow and we'll hit the bull's-eye—every time!

5. Are we famous? Ever heard of amazon.com or the Amazon River?

4. Wonder Woman is based on us.

3. We go to extreme lengths to shoot well.

2. For his ninth labor, Heracles took Queen Hippolyte's golden belt.

1. We make the Greek heroes shake in their sandals.

Family, Flings, Friends, and Foes

▼ Parents	▼ Siblings	▼ Offspring	▼ Friends	▼ Foes		
Ares and Otero	Harmonia	Hippolytus	Artemis	Achilles	Heracles	Theseus

The AMAZONS

WANTED: WOMEN WARRIORS

Calling all females—it's girl-power time! We're on the warpath and we want YOU to join us! So leave that bumbling boyfriend behind and join us on a road-trip rampage to rescue our sister-soldier Antiope and get back our mighty queen's magic belt. (We'll show Heracles what happens when a mere man messes with the brave and bold Amazons!) Are you handy with a bow and arrow—and ready to show the boys who's boss? Then we want you! Girly-girls need not apply.

REALITY CHECK

How did the Amazon rain forest get its name? Spanish and Portuguese conquerors searching for gold and silver in South America claimed to have seen "tall women warriors." The Spanish named them Amazons, after the female warriors of Greek mythology, and their name was given to that area.

I owe it all to the Amazons.

Rain forest

Bellerophon   Dionysus

Wonder Woman

Αμαζον

HERE'S LOOKING AT YOU

The Amazons were a race of women warriors who lived in Anatolia (formerly Asia Minor) and fought with the Trojans against the Greeks in the Trojan War. During the war, their queen, Penthesileia, was killed by the Greek hero Achilles. In fact, many Greek heroes fought against the Amazons. Heracles had to obtain the belt of Queen Hippolyte as one of his twelve labors; Theseus kidnapped Queen Antiope (some stories say Hippolyte), who gave birth to his son Hippolytus; Bellerophon had to fight them and escaped with his life astride Pegasus, the **immortal** winged horse; and Dionysus, the god of wine and revelry, conquered them as part of his exploits.

HIPPOLYTE'S BELT

A hero battles for a prize belt.

The goddess Hera, wife of the mighty god Zeus, had been out to kill Heracles since his birth to her husband's girlfriend Alcmene. Hera finally caused the mighty hero to lose his mind. In his madness, Heracles killed his own wife and children. When he came to his senses and realized what he'd done, Heracles asked the god Apollo for guidance. Through his **oracle**, Apollo assigned Heracles twelve labors, or extremely difficult tasks, to perform for King Eurystheus. The ninth labor was to retrieve a gold belt the god Ares had given to his daughter Hippolyte, queen of the Amazons.

When Heracles and his crew arrived at the land of the Amazons, Hippolyte promised to give him the belt. But Hera convinced the women that Heracles had come to kill their queen. The Amazons attacked Heracles and his crew. Heracles, believing that he had been betrayed by Hippolyte, killed her and took the belt. Upon his return home, he gave the belt to Eurystheus.

Amazons vs. Athenians

THE ABDUCTION OF ANTIOPE

Antiope gets carried away and the Amazons look for a fight.

After Heracles retrieved Ares' belt from Hippolyte, his companion Theseus wanted to take something home as a **memento**. So he kidnapped Antiope, an Amazon queen, and took her back to Athens as his bride. There she bore him a son, Hippolytus.

In the meantime, the Amazons were fighting mad about their queen's capture, so they followed Theseus to Athens and engaged the Athenians in battle. When Theseus later abandoned Antiope and married Phaedra, the daughter of King Minos of Crete, Antiope and the other Amazons stormed Athens.

REALITY CHECK
Wonder Woman, a famous female superhero, can trace her origins to the mythical Amazons. She comes from an all-female tribe of warriors just like the ancient Amazons. Her mother was even named Queen Hippolyte.

Want to know more? Go to:
http://www.dccomics.com/sites/wonderwoman/

"You always hurt the one you love …"

Wonder Woman

PENTHESILEIA AND ACHILLES

The Amazons throw down in the Trojan War.

The Trojan War was fought between the Greeks and the Trojans. The fighting took place in the city of Troy. Not wanting to miss a good **skirmish**, the Amazons joined the war as allies of the Trojans. They were led by Penthesileia, a daughter of the war god Ares. The Amazons were brave warriors and had much success on the battlefield. But when Penthesileia met the Greek hero Achilles in hand-to-hand combat, it was all over for the Amazon. Achilles killed her—but not before falling in love with her for her brains, beauty, and courage. Achilles made sure Penthesileia was given a proper burial. He even killed one of his men who'd teased him about his crush on the Amazon.

REALITY CHECK
Was the Trojan War real? Archaeologists believe that the story of the war was probably based on actual historical events of the early twelfth century BCE.

yo a–
u fight like a boy. is
that the best u can do? c u
on the battlefield 2morrow.
if u don't show up, i'm gonna
tell every-1 what a chicken
u r. P.

↓ Profile of Balius and Xanthus

Sounds Like: bay´-li-us; zan´-thuss

Generation:
☐ Titan
☑ Olympian
☑ Other: Immortal horses

Special Abilities: Prophecy
Speech
Speed

Characteristics: Immortality

Top 10 Things to Know About Us:

10. Sure, we look like regular horses, but we can run like the wind—and talk.

9. Poseidon gave us to Achilles' father, Peleus, as a wedding present.

8. We were Achilles' chariot horses during the Trojan War.

7. We are immortal.

6. Our dear, gentle father, Zephyrus, is the god of the warm west wind.

5. Our mother, Podarge, is—let's face it—a Harpy.

4. It's not every day you meet horses that can predict the future.

3. We don't mind pulling Achilles' chariot, but we'd much rather chat with him.

2. We cried like babies when Achilles' friend Patroclus died.

1. Our master, Achilles, is one of the greatest Greek heroes.

Hey, where's the party?

Hay? Where's the hay?

↓ Family, Flings, Friends, and Foes

▼ Parents	▼ Siblings	▼ Friends				▼ Foes
Zephyrus and Podarge	Carpus	Achilles	Peleus	Patroclus	Hera	The Furies

BALIUS and XANTHUS
FAST TALKERS

What are *you* staring at? Haven't you ever seen talking horses before? No? Then go ahead and stare. Take a good long look. Note to a certain hero: There are better ways to spend your *last day alive*—oops! Did we say that aloud? Never mind! Nothing to worry about! It's not like we can *tell the future*! Sorry if we got off on the wrong hoof. Can we give you a ride into battle? Hop into our chariot—and hang on tight!

Hey, I saw the future first!

Mr. Ed

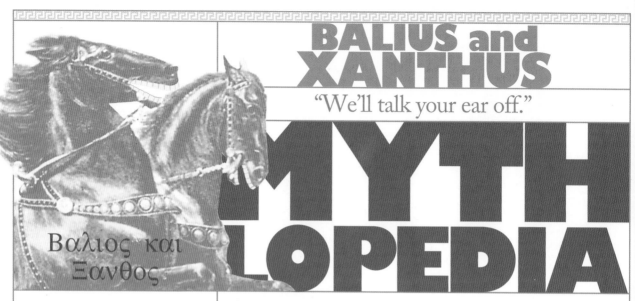

BALIUS and XANTHUS

"We'll talk your ear off."

MYTHLOPEDIA

Βαλιος και Ξανθος

HERE'S TALKING TO YOU

With the following words, Xanthus warns Achilles that his death is near. But it will not be the fault of the horses—it has been determined by a god and fate.

> "We shall still keep you safe for this time, o hard [Achilles]. And yet the day of your death is near, but it is not we who are to blame, but a great god and powerful Destiny."
> —Homer, *The Iliad*, Book XIX

Xanthus

Balius

GIFT HORSES

The god of the sea gives an unusual wedding gift. When Peleus, a member of the **Argonauts** and a warrior and adventurer (later the father of the great Greek hero Achilles), and the sea **nymph** Thetis got married, they invited some Mount Olympus VIGs (very important gods) to attend the celebration. Poseidon, the powerful god of the sea, presented the couple with a unique wedding present: two **immortal** horses. Named Balius and Xanthus, these two speedy steeds were the offspring of Zephyrus, the god of the warm west wind, and Podarge, a Harpy and the stormy wind. It came as no surprise that these horses could run as fast as the wind. But the horses had an amazing gift of their own that would be revealed later!

"We were definitely the best wedding presents."

Hector
Balius
Achilles
Xanthus
Patroclus

FRESH HORSES

Achilles takes his trusty steeds to the Trojan War and they speak their minds.

When the hero Achilles went to fight with the Greeks in the Trojan War, he took Balius and Xanthus, his father's immortal horses, to pull his **chariot**.

During the war Achilles captured a young Trojan girl as his servant. When General Agamemnon ordered Achilles to give up the girl, Achilles stormed off the battlefield in a huff and refused to fight.

Without their hero, the Greeks began to lose. So Patroclus, Achilles' best friend, borrowed Achilles' armor and chariot and headed off into battle. Soon word came back that the Trojan prince Hector had killed Patroclus. Achilles was **distraught**—and angry. He berated his horses for allowing Patroclus to die and leaving his body on the battlefield. The horses were outraged that Achilles would think such a thing. The goddess Hera enabled Xanthus to speak, and he reminded Achilles that the god of **prophecy**, Apollo, had foretold of Patroclus's death. He also told Achilles that his death had been foretold, too. But before Xanthus could say another word, the Furies— three sisters whose role was to pursue and punish criminals— shut him up!

REALITY CHECK

Today, the term *Achilles' heel* is used to describe a person's weakness. And the Achilles **tendon** joins the bone in your heel to your calf muscle.

MYTHING LINK

Achilles was the strongest, swiftest, and most capable of the Greek heroes. When Achilles was a baby, his mother wanted to protect him from all mortal wounds, so she held him by his heel and dipped him in the River Styx. From then on, his whole body was **invincible**, except for the spot where she had held him.

Thetis

Baby Achilles

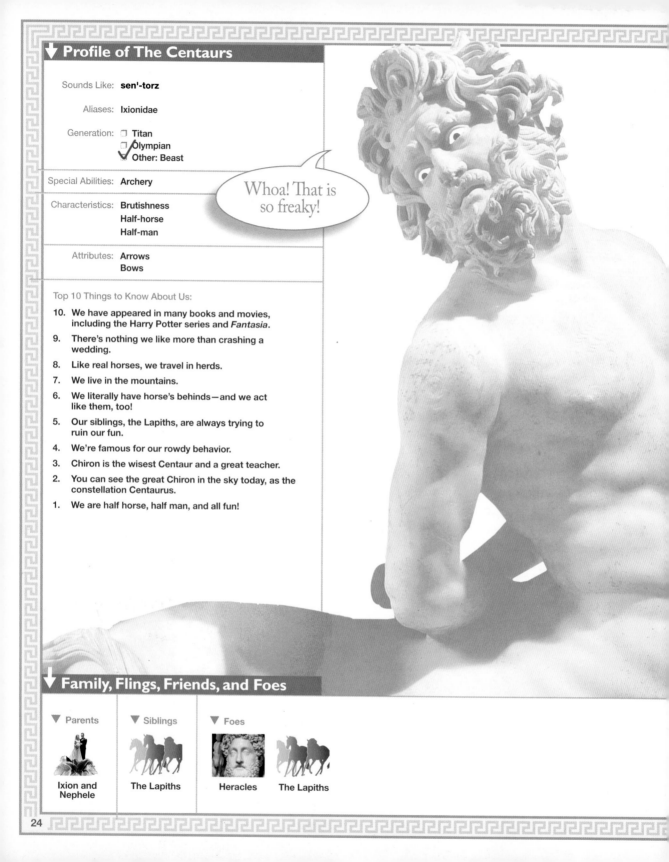

▼ Profile of The Centaurs

Sounds Like:	**sen'-torz**
Aliases:	Ixionidae
Generation:	☐ Titan ☑ Olympian ☐ Other: Beast
Special Abilities:	**Archery**
Characteristics:	**Brutishness** **Half-horse** **Half-man**
Attributes:	**Arrows** **Bows**

Whoa! That is so freaky!

Top 10 Things to Know About Us:

10. We have appeared in many books and movies, including the Harry Potter series and *Fantasia*.

9. There's nothing we like more than crashing a wedding.

8. Like real horses, we travel in herds.

7. We live in the mountains.

6. We literally have horse's behinds—and we act like them, too!

5. Our siblings, the Lapiths, are always trying to ruin our fun.

4. We're famous for our rowdy behavior.

3. Chiron is the wisest Centaur and a great teacher.

2. You can see the great Chiron in the sky today, as the constellation Centaurus.

1. We are half horse, half man, and all fun!

▼ Family, Flings, Friends, and Foes

▼ Parents	▼ Siblings	▼ Foes	
Ixion and Nephele	The Lapiths	Heracles	The Lapiths

The CENTAURS
SCHOOL FOR SCOUNDRELS

Welcome, Centaurs, to Manners 101. I am Professor Chiron, renowned teacher of gods and heroes. You're here because— Stop that! We don't make rude noises when the teacher is speaking. As I was saying— Hey! Keep your hooves to yourselves; I don't care who started it. Now, since I'm the only half man, half horse— Halt! No stampeding in the classroom! You're acting like animals! I won't tolerate horseplay in this classroom!

Excuse me. I think I got the wrong head.

REALITY CHECK

NASA developed the Centaur Rocket, a booster rocket for launching other spacecraft into space, in the late 1950s and early 1960s. Known as America's workhorse in space, it was fueled by liquid oxygen and liquid hydrogen.

Want to know more? Go to:
http://www.nasa.gov/
centers/glenn/about/his-
tory/centaur.html

Κενταυροι

The CENTAURS

"Are you ready to rock?"

MYTH LOPEDIA

Centaur

HERE'S LOOKING AT YOU

If you were to see a Centaur head on, you might not realize at first that you were looking at a magical creature. With the torso and head of a man, a Centaur looked pretty normal from the front … but once he turned to the side, there'd be no doubt as to what he was. It's hard to hide a horse's behind!

"Mom was as delicate as a cloud and Dad as stubborn as a mule. What a pair!"

A CLOUDY START
The first Centaur is born.

The Lapiths lived high up in the mountains of Thessaly. They were unruly people: When they saw something they wanted, they just took it.

Their king, Ixion, was in love with the goddess Hera and wanted her for himself. There was just one catch—Hera was the wife of Zeus, the mighty ruler of the gods. When Hera told Zeus that Ixion had a crush on her, Zeus decided to teach Ixion a lesson. The powerful god molded Nephele, a phantom made of a cloud, in Hera's image and placed it near Ixion. Mistaking the cloud for the goddess, Ixion showered it with affection. Enraged that Ixion would attempt to steal his wife,

Zeus sent Ixion whirling through the air on a flaming wheel—but not before Ixion and Nephele had become the proud parents of a bouncing baby half-boy, half-horse. This baby, named Centaurus, was the first Centaur.

REALITY CHECK

In the Harry Potter series, Centaurs live in the Forbidden Forest and, except for a Centaur named Firenze, don't like humans. He's friends with Dumbledore and teaches divination at Hogwarts School.

WEDDING CRASHERS
The Centaurs ruin the fun for everyone.

Ixion's son Pirithous, the new king of the Lapiths, was getting married to Hippodamia. The Lapiths' wild relatives, the Centaurs, attended the wedding. Talk about bad behavior!

The Centaurs galloped through the wedding creating total **mayhem**, annoying all the women—including the bride, drinking all the punch, and gulping down all the food. As if that weren't bad enough, the Centaurs and the Lapiths began to brawl. Fortunately, the Centaurs were too exhausted to put up a good fight and they were quickly subdued. From that time on, they were banished from Thessaly.

> "It was quite a party!"

CHIRON'S HONOR ROLL
CHIRON'S STUDENTS WENT ON TO DO GREAT THINGS. HERE ARE SOME OF THEIR ACCOMPLISHMENTS:

➤ JASON: LEADER OF THE ARGONAUTS AND HERO WHO STOLE THE GOLDEN FLEECE.

➤ ACHILLES: THE GREATEST GREEK HERO OF THE TROJAN WAR. HE WAS NEARLY INVINCIBLE, EXCEPT FOR A WEAK SPOT IN HIS HEEL.

➤ HERACLES: THE STRONGEST, MOST COURAGEOUS OF ALL GREEK HEROES. HE DEFEATED CERBERUS, THE NEMEAN LION, AND HYDRA, TO NAME A FEW.

➤ ASCLEPIUS: THE GOD OF HEALING, WHO COULD BRING THE DEAD BACK TO LIFE.

➤ THESEUS: THE ATHENIAN PRINCE WHO KILLED THE MINOTAUR AND MADE ATHENS A GREAT CITY.

CHIRON: A DIFFERENT KIND OF CENTAUR
There's one in every bunch.

Chiron was a wise, kind, and knowledgeable Centaur who stood apart from the rest of his beastly brothers. In some stories Chiron was a half brother of the mighty god Zeus and not even related to the other Centaurs, but he had the misfortune to look like them. His father was the Titan Cronus and his mother was a **nymph** named Philyra. He was an uncle to Apollo and Artemis, who taught Chiron many arts, including medicine and science. He, in turn, passed on some of that knowledge to such Greek heroes and scholars as Jason, Achilles, and Heracles, and to Apollo's son Asclepius.

Centaurs · Lapiths

THE DEATH OF CHIRON

Even heroes make mistakes sometimes.

The great hero Heracles was visiting Thessaly when he got into an argument with a group of Centaurs. One thing led to another, and soon a full-blown brawl erupted. Chiron, the wise Centaur, was in the area at the time and got caught in the crossfire. One of Heracles' arrows hit Chiron in the knee. Although the wound wasn't deep, the tip of the arrow that caused it had been dipped in the poisonous blood of Hydra, a hideous monster. Heracles was horrified that he'd wounded the great Chiron, but there was nothing he could do for the ailing creature. Because he was

Hydra's blood

immortal, Chiron couldn't die from the wound but he was in agony. Desperate to end his misery, Chiron gave up his immortality to Prometheus, who'd stolen fire from gods and given it to mortals. When Chiron finally died, Zeus placed the beloved teacher in the heavens as the constellation now known as Centaurus.

REALITY CHECK

A Centaur was also part of the constellation Sagittarius, which can be seen from the Northern Hemisphere in the summer. The stars in the constellation form the shape of a Centaur shooting Scorpius, the scorpion, with a bow and arrow.

Want to know more? Go to: http://www.enchantedlearning.com/subjects/ astronomy/stars/constellations.shtml

Hydra

Heracles

The Constellation Sagittarius

"Zeus put me out of my misery and into the sky."

THE DEATH OF HERACLES

A hero is bested by a Centaur.

When he was a young man, the mighty hero Heracles went temporarily insane and accidentally killed his wife, Megara. To pay for his crime, Heracles had to perform twelve labors that had been devised by the Greek king Eurystheus. The labors ranged from killing the fierce Nemean Lion to cleaning out the Augean stables to fetching Cerberus, the vicious guard dog of the gates to the **Underworld**.

After Heracles successfully completed the labors, he finally settled down with the lovely Deianeira. One day, as Heracles and his honey were on a journey, she was abducted by a brutish Centaur named Nessus. Heracles tracked down the **rogue** Centaur and shot him with an arrow that had been dipped in Hydra's poisonous blood. As the beast lay dying, he gave Deianeira his bloody shirt. He told her that if Heracles should ever fall out of love with her, she should give him the shirt to wear and it would reignite his passion.

In time, Deianeira began to suspect that her husband might be losing interest in her. So she took the Centaur's shirt and gave it to Heracles to wear.

When Heracles put on the shirt, he was burned by the fiery blood. The hero wanted to die to escape the pain. In agony, he threw himself on a lit **pyre**.

His immortal part rose up to Mount Olympus, where he became reconciled with Hera, who had wanted to kill him out of revenge because he was the son of Hera's husband and his girlfriend Alcmene. The hero lives on in the heavens as the constellation Heracles.

Ouch!

Heracles

Centaur

Get this to a laundromat!

Profile of Cerberus

Sounds Like: sur'-bur-uhs

Aliases: Watchdog of Hades

Generation:
- ☐ Titan
- ☐ Olympian
- ☑ Other: Monster

Special Abilities: Guarding the gates of the Underworld

Characteristics: Sharp claws
Snake's tail
Three barking, snarling heads

Attributes: Snakes coiled around necks

Top 10 Things to Know About Me:

10. I might look tough, but a good lullaby makes me sleep like a puppy.

9. My family reunions make your Halloween party look tame.

8. My father almost stole Zeus's kingdom. I could have been a royal hound.

7. I went to the upperworld once … thanks to Heracles.

6. I inspired one of the characters in the Harry Potter series—Hagrid's three-headed dog, Fluffy.

5. Even some of today's biggest dog breeds, like Great Danes and mastiffs, are puny compared to me.

4. My saliva is rumored to have produced aconite, a poisonous plant also known as wolfsbane.

3. My master, Hades, is the god of the Underworld. When he says sit, I sit.

2. I have three words of advice: BEWARE OF DOG.

1. If my bark doesn't get you, my bite surely will.

> Woof, woof, woof …

Family, Flings, Friends, and Foes

▼ Parents

Typhon and Echidna

▼ Siblings

The Nemean Lion

The Chimera

Hydra

The Sphinx

▼ Friends

Hades

Charon

CERBERUS

IT'S A DOG'S LIFE

WOOF! I can't believe I have to go to obedience school just because I fell asleep on the job. I was a *great* guard dog until Orpheus played that lullaby on his lyre. There's so much I do right. I can fetch and play dead. I don't even chase chariots! And with three heads, my bark is definitely not worse than my bite. Hades can't rule the Underworld without me. *Arrooooooooo*!

Oh no, not again!

REALITY CHECK

Many characters in Greek mythology have planets, moons, or other celestial bodies named for them. Cerberus is no exception. An asteroid discovered in 1971 by astronomer Lubos Kohoutek is named for this mythological guard dog.

Want to know more? Go to: http://solarsystem.nasa.gov/planets/profile.cfm?Object=Asteroids

Cerberus asteroid

▼ Foes

Heracles   **Orpheus**

CERBERUS

"Who let the dogs out?"

MYTHLOPEDIA

Κερβερος

HERE'S LOOKING AT YOU

Cerberus was the three-headed guard dog at the gates of the **Underworld**. His job was to keep dead souls from escaping. One look at the beastly canine, and it's easy to see why he was successful. Each of his three heads had a mouth full of gnashing teeth and snakes wrapped around its neck. His paws ended in razor-sharp claws, and he had a serpent's tail!

BEWARE of DOG

THE CAPTURE OF CERBERUS

Heracles visits the Underworld and returns with a puppy!

Heracles' twelfth and final labor was perhaps his hardest—he had to capture Cerberus from the Underworld and take him to the world of the living. First, Heracles asked the god of the Underworld, Hades, for permission. Hades agreed on the condition that Heracles not use any weapons to capture his loyal dog. So Heracles wrestled Cerberus. It was a close match—hero versus multiheaded hound—but Heracles won and carried the three-headed beast to the upperworld. As soon as King Eurystheus, who had come up with the twelve labors, saw Cerberus, he told Heracles to return the dog to Hades. Cerberus was too vicious to be among the living!

REALITY CHECK

With proper training, several breeds of dog can make excellent guard dogs, including Tibetan mastiffs, boxers, German shepherds, and Doberman pinschers.

Want to know more? Go to: http://www.akc.org/ breeds/working_group.cfm

Doberman Pinschers

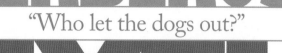

Your eyes are getting heavy ... heavy ...

ROCK-A-BYE PUPPY

Orpheus tiptoes past Cerberus but leaves his love behind.

Orpheus was the best musician in Greece. The music he played on his **lyre** was even more beautiful than the haunting tunes of the Sirens, three singing **nymphs** whose mystical songs lured sailors to their doom.

But Orpheus was sad. His wife, Eurydice, was dead and gone. Determined to bring her back, Orpheus made his way toward the Underworld. First he had to get past Cerberus, who guarded the gates and prevented the dead from leaving. As he approached the snarling watchdog, Orpheus played a tune on his lyre. It was so lovely that it lulled Cerberus to sleep, allowing Orpheus to sneak past him. Hades and Persephone, the king and queen of the Underworld, were so moved by the music that they agreed to allow Orpheus take Eurydice back to the land of the living on one condition—he could not look at her until they were back on Earth. Orpheus led his dead wife's soul toward the gate but as they drew near, he took a quick glance back at Eurydice. Snap! She went straight back to the Underworld and Orpheus lost her forever.

REALITY CHECK

Does something sound familiar in the story of Orpheus going to the Underworld to retrieve his dead wife? In *Harry Potter and the Sorcerer's Stone*, Hagrid's giant, three-headed dog, Fluffy, guards the entrance to the hiding place of the sacred stone. The only way to get past him is by playing music that will make him fall asleep.

Want to know more? Go to: http://www.hp-encyclopedia.com/characters.php?page=charactersf

MYTHING LINK

The Underworld, or realm of the dead, was ruled by Hades, a brother of the powerful gods Zeus and Poseidon, and his queen, Persephone. It was separated from the world of the living by the River Styx.

New arrivals were ferried across the Styx by Charon. While unwelcome visitors were prevented from entering the Underworld by Cerberus, the beast's primary job was keeping dead souls in.

Once a soul had entered the Underworld, it would be assigned a place to spend eternity: the Elysian Fields, Tartarus, or the Meadows of Asphodel.

The Underworld

Profile of The Chimera

Sounds Like: ki-meer'-uh

Generation: ☐ Titan
☐ Olympian
☑ Other: Monster

Special Abilities: Breathing fire

Characteristics: Goat's head
Lion's head and body
Serpent's tail

> Does anybody have a breath mint?

Top 10 Things to Know About Me:

10. Causing mayhem for the people of Lycia is my favorite pastime.

9. If you ask me, Bellerophon got what was coming to him. He was always riding mighty high.

8. What do you get when you cross a lion, a goat, and a snake? You're looking at it!

7. If I had a pair of wings instead of an extra head, that pesky Bellerophon would have been toast.

6. Say my name today and you might be talking about any number of monsters, especially imaginary ones.

5. Many writers have compared my fire-breathing skills to a volcano.

4. You can find fish named after me in the ocean today. They're also known as ghost sharks.

3. Some people think I was born on a volcano where lions, goats, and snakes all lived.

2. My home, Lycia, is now a part of Turkey.

1. Don't get too close. I'm a hothead!

Family, Flings, Friends, and Foes

▼ Parents

Typhon and Echidna

▼ Siblings

The Nemean Lion

Cerberus

Hydra

The Sphinx

▼ Foes

Bellerophon

Pegasus

King Iobates

The CHIMERA

LETTER FROM CAMP

Dear Mom and Dad,

How are you? Camp Mighty Monster is great! For once, I'm really fitting in. I don't stand out around here, even with my lion head, goat body, and snake tail! And my fire breathing comes in handy for roasting hot dogs! My counselor is named Medusa and she rocks! She gave me some great tips for styling my mane. I gotta go—it's time for s'mores. After that, I have a city to ravage.

Love,
Chimera

Chimera of Arezzo

35

The CHIMERA

"There's a fire in my belly!"

MYTH LOPEDIA

Χημαιρα

HERE'S LOOKING AT YOU!

The Chimera, a fire-breathing monster, **ravaged** the countryside around Lycia. Talk about killer looks! This female creature had the head, mane, and body of a lion, a goat's head on its back, and a serpent as a tail!

The Chimera was a mixture of these animals in one big, fluffy ball of fun!

TROUBLE IN THE NEIGHBORHOOD

A hero handles a challenge with the help of a horse.

The ferocious Chimera had been tormenting the people of Lycia. She attacked women, children, and livestock, leaving behind nothing but piles of bones. The people were helpless in the face of the fire-breathing monster.

Meanwhile, the hero Bellerophon was visiting King Proteus of Argos. The king's wife, Anteia, flirted with the hunky hero, but he ignored her advances. This angered the queen, so she told her husband that Bellerophon had been flirting with her. Furious, the king handed Bellerophon a sealed letter and told him to deliver it—unopened!—to Iobates of Lycia.

When Iobates opened the letter, it read, "Kill the bearer of this letter." So Iobates challenged Bellerophon to a series of tasks that were designed to kill him. The first task was to kill the Chimera.

As he made his way toward Lycia, Bellerophon—with the goddess Athena's help—captured and tamed the winged horse Pegasus. As the pair confronted the Chimera, the beast roared, spewed fire, stabbed at them with her horns, and swiped with her claws. But Pegasus was too quick and agile for the beast. As Pegasus hovered above the monster, Bellerophon drove his long spear into her heart and killed her.

CHIMERA GETS THE LAST LAUGH

A cocky hero goes for a ride and flies off his horse.

After Bellerophon killed the Chimera, he successfully completed several other tasks given to him by Iobates. Impressed with Bellerophon's bravery, Iobates allowed the hero to marry his daughter Philonoe. The couple had three children.

By now, Bellerophon was a bit full of himself, so he decided to jump astride Pegasus and visit the gods on Mount Olympus. When Zeus, the mighty ruler of the gods, saw the arrogant hero headed his way, he sent a fly to punish Bellerophon. The fly stung Pegasus, causing the horse to throw its rider. Bellerophon plunged to the ground.

Although Bellerophon's life was saved by the goddess Athena, he spent the rest of his days wandering, lonely and confused, looking for Pegasus.

Fire-breathing Dragon

MYTHING LINK

Fire-breathing dragons have lived in people's imaginations for thousands of years. The idea of dragons may have developed out of primitive human fears of dangerous animals, such as large snakes and birds of prey. Dragons may have also been inspired by early discoveries of the fossils of extinct animals. For example, many fossil dinosaur skulls found in China resemble the dragons depicted in ancient Chinese art. In Europe, fossils of huge cave bears were found surrounded by heaps of smaller bones. This may have led to tales of great dragons lurking in caves and preying on humans.

"Some like it hot!"

Bellerophon

Pegasus

The Chimera

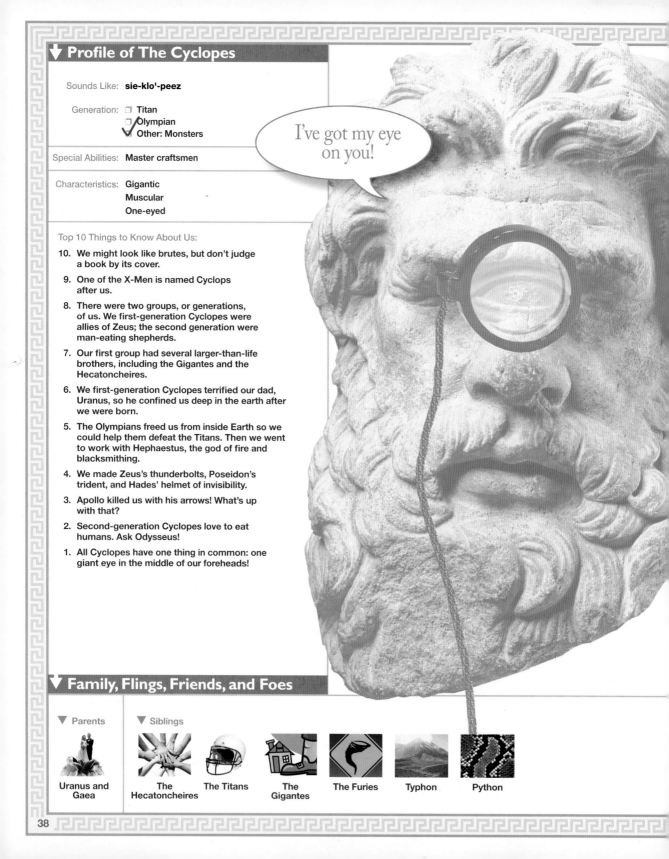

▼ Profile of The Cyclopes

Sounds Like: **sie-klo'-peez**

Generation: ☐ Titan
☐ Olympian
☑ Other: Monsters

Special Abilities: **Master craftsmen**

Characteristics: **Gigantic**
Muscular
One-eyed

I've got my eye on you!

Top 10 Things to Know About Us:

10. We might look like brutes, but don't judge a book by its cover.

9. One of the X-Men is named Cyclops after us.

8. There were two groups, or generations, of us. We first-generation Cyclopes were allies of Zeus; the second generation were man-eating shepherds.

7. Our first group had several larger-than-life brothers, including the Gigantes and the Hecatoncheires.

6. We first-generation Cyclopes terrified our dad, Uranus, so he confined us deep in the earth after we were born.

5. The Olympians freed us from inside Earth so we could help them defeat the Titans. Then we went to work with Hephaestus, the god of fire and blacksmithing.

4. We made Zeus's thunderbolts, Poseidon's trident, and Hades' helmet of invisibility.

3. Apollo killed us with his arrows! What's up with that?

2. Second-generation Cyclopes love to eat humans. Ask Odysseus!

1. All Cyclopes have one thing in common: one giant eye in the middle of our foreheads!

▼ Family, Flings, Friends, and Foes

▼ Parents	▼ Siblings					
Uranus and Gaea	The Hecatoncheires	The Titans	The Gigantes	The Furies	Typhon	Python

The CYCLOPES

MUSCLE MONSTERS

We know we're not easy on the eye (or, in your case, *eyes*). But what we lack in eyeballs we make up for in muscles! Have you seen our delts? Our abs? You could bounce a drachma off our six-packs. We are *cut*. And that's good, because it takes a strong monster to make those thunderbolts for Zeus. Don't hate us because we're built—or because of what we've built. Beauty is in the (one) eye of the beholder!

REALITY CHECK

Since he first appeared in the 1960s, Cyclops has been one of the main characters of *The X-Men*. Inspired by the Greek Cyclopes, he wears a special visor that makes him look like he has one eye.

Want to know more? Go to: http://www.marvel.com/ universeCyclops_%28Scott_ Summers%29

X-Man Cyclops

Poseidon

This trident rocks!

▼ Friends

Zeus   Hephaestus   Poseidon   Hades

▼ Foes

Apollo   Oedipus

Κυκλωψ

The CYCLOPES

"Beauty is in the eye of the beholder."

MYTHLOPEDIA

HERE'S LOOKING AT YOU

Why was the Cyclopes' father, Uranus, so afraid of them? Huge and muscular, with only a single eye each, these giants were a fearsome sight! They were also known to be violent, powerful, and stubborn—not exactly the ideal sons!

Some believe that Cyclopes were described as having only one eye because in ancient times **blacksmiths** often wore a patch over one eye to protect it from flying sparks. If the unprotected eye got burned, a blacksmith would still be able to see.

"We ruled in shop class."

WHAT A FAMILY!
Grumpy dads run in the family.

The first Cyclopes were the three sons of Uranus (sky) and Gaea (earth). Their names were Brontes (thunder), Steropes (lightning), and Arges (brightness). Gaea and Uranus were also the parents of the Hecatoncheires (hundred-handed giants) and the Titans. Uranus hated his children. He imprisoned them in Tartarus, the deepest part of the **Underworld**. This caused Gaea much pain. At her urging, the youngest Titan, Cronus, attacked his father and released all the Titans from Tartarus.

When Cronus became a father, he feared that his children would one day challenge him, so he swallowed each baby as it was born. But when his mate Rhea gave birth to Zeus, she hid the baby and tricked Cronus into swallowing a stone in his place. Eventually Zeus returned and freed his siblings, the Olympians. Then he released the Cyclopes and Hecatoncheires and led them all in a battle against the Titans.

REALITY CHECK
The walls of several ancient cities, made of massive, irregular stones, are known as Cyclopean works. They date from about 3000 BCE to 700 BCE. The term came into use because of the ancient belief that the structures had been built by the Cyclopes of Greek myth. Beyond Greece, similar walls can be found in Italy, Peru, the Middle East, and Asia.

MAKING THE GOODS FOR THE GODS

Zeus gets some powerful weapons in return for freeing the Cyclopes.

The first-generation Cyclopes became the blacksmiths of the gods. They supplied the weapons that were used to defeat Cronus and the Titans. For Zeus, the Cyclopes crafted thunderbolts that he used against his enemies. For Hades, god of the Underworld, they made a helmet of invisibility. The hero Perseus used this helmet when he set out to kill the monstrous Gorgon Medusa. For Poseidon, god of the sea, they made a **trident**. By slamming his trident against the ground, Poseidon created earthquakes; he also used it to call forth storms and giant ocean waves.

Helmet of invisibility

Thunderbolt

WEAPONS OF THE GODS

Trident

DEATH OF THE CYCLOPES

Apollo gets mad at Zeus and takes it out on the Cyclopes.

Apollo's son Asclepius had been taught the art of medicine by Chiron, a wise Centaur. Asclepius was such a skilled healer that the goddess Athena had given him a **vial** of Gorgon blood, which he could use to bring the dead back to life. This enraged Hades, the god of the Underworld, since he was the ruler of dead souls. Hades complained to the mighty Zeus,

ruler of the gods, who had a solution: He killed Asclepius with a thunderbolt!

Distraught, Apollo used his bow and arrows to shoot and kill the Cyclopes who'd crafted Zeus's thunderbolts. Finally, to make amends with Apollo for killing his son and to show appreciation for Asclepius's medical skills, Zeus turned Asclepius into a constellation, Ophiuchus, the Serpent Bearer.

Apollo

Cyclops

"You try to do a god a favor and look where it gets you ... a whole lotta dead!"

MEET OTHER ONE-EYED BEASTS

Michael "Mike" Wazowski, of *Monsters Inc.* fame, is a tennis-ball-shaped monster with one big eye, and horns on top of his head. As a scare assistant, he provides closet doors for his partner to hide behind and scare children.

Basilisk, of Marvel Comics' *New X Men,* is a one-eyed, bald, and grotesquely large mutant.

Kang and Kodos, familiar to fans of *The Simpsons*, are one-eyed aliens from the planet Rigel VII.

These are my peeps!

Turanga Leela is a cyclops-like sewer mutant and star of the TV series *Futurama*.

Agent Wendy Pleakley, of Disney's *Lilo & Stitch*, is a Plorgonarian who works for the Galactic Federation.

B.O.B. (Benzoate Ostylezene Bicarbonate), a brainless, one-eyed, bloblike mass from *Monsters vs. Aliens*, was created as a result of an industrial accident at a snack-food plant.

HAPPY WITH HEPHAESTUS

The Cyclopes' spirits live beneath Mount Etna, where they help Hephaestus.

After Apollo killed the Cyclopes, their spirits were placed beneath Mount Etna in Sicily, where they became the helpers of Hephaestus, the god of fire and blacksmithing. There, they forged shields, swords, arrows, **chariots**, and other tools and wondrous objects for the gods of Olympus.

Today the smoke that comes forth from Mount Etna, still an active volcano, is said to come from the fires of the Cyclopes' burning forges.

The Cyclopes made these for Zeus!

thunderbolts

A HERO DROPS BY

Odysseus comes eye to eye with a Cyclops.

The clever hero Odysseus had faced some frightening challenges by the time he encountered the second-generation Cyclopes. Also one-eyed giants, these Cyclopes were **barbaric** cave-dwellers and offspring of the sea god Poseidon.

Odysseus had fought with the Greeks in the Trojan War. With the goddess Athena's help, he came up with the scheme of using a wooden horse, which led to the fall of Troy and victory for the Greeks. But the challenges Odysseus had faced at Troy were small compared to his **arduous** ten-year journey home to Ithaca after the war.

As Odysseus and his men sailed home, they stopped on an island off the coast of present-day Italy for supplies. Once ashore, the men took shelter in a cave. What they didn't know was that the cave belonged to a ferocious Cyclops named Polyphemus, who was out tending his sheep.

When Polyphemus returned home and found Odysseus and his crew in the cave, he blocked the entrance so they couldn't escape. That was just the beginning.

Odysseus

Polyphemus

unlucky sailors

A DRAMATIC ESCAPE

Polyphemus is still hungry.

Polyphemus had just one thought when he found Odysseus and his crew in his cave: dinner! So the hungry Cyclops gobbled up two men. The next morning, the Cyclops ate two men for breakfast, and two more for lunch. Desperate to avoid becoming another snack for the hungry beast, Odysseus struck up a conversation with Polyphemus. The clever hero told the Cyclops that his name was No Man. While Odysseus continued to talk, Polyphemus, his belly full of sailors, fell sound asleep.

Cautiously, Odysseus retrieved a spear that he and his men had carved earlier in the day. As Polyphemus lay sleeping, Odysseus stabbed him in the eye with the spear, blinding the beast. The Cyclops shrieked in pain, causing other Cyclopes on the island to come running. Polyphemus cried out that No Man had blinded him. Hearing this, the other Cyclopes assumed that Polyphemus must have done something to offend the gods, so they went away.

The next morning, when Polyphemus opened the cave, Odysseus and his crew hid among the sheep and escaped.

Mmmm. Lunch!

▼ Profile of The Gigantes

Sounds Like: **jie'-gan-teez**

Aliases: **Giants**

Generation: ☐ Titan
☐ Olympian
☑ Other: Monsters

Special Abilities: **Causing earthquakes and volcanic eruptions**
Throwing heavy objects

Characteristics: **Serpent legs**

Attributes: **Rocks**
Spears
Torches

Do you have anything in XXXXXXXXXL?

Top 10 Things to Know About Us:

10. We battled the Olympians after they defeated the Titans, but before they took on the monster Typhon.

9. The Olympians challenged us when we tried to overtake Mount Olympus.

8. Athena killed a bunch of us, including Pallas, who had the skin of a goat.

7. We aren't the only giants of myth and legend; many other cultures have stories about giants.

6. Twenty-four of us were born from the blood of our father, Uranus, when it fell on our mother, Gaea.

5. If not for Heracles, we would rule the world.

4. We are buried underneath volcanoes.

3. Our second-in-command, Enkelados, was killed by Athena and now lies under Mount Etna in Sicily.

2. Only Aristaeus survived the war with the gods; he's now a dung beetle!

1. At home our king, Alcyoneus, was immortal so Heracles dragged him away to die.

▼ Family, Flings, Friends, and Foes

▼ Parents

Uranus and Gaea

▼ Siblings

The Hecatoncheires   **The Titans**   **The Cyclopes**   **The Furies**   **Python**   **Typhon**

▼ Foes

The Olympians   **Heracles**

The GIGANTES
BIG LOSERS

Mom-m-m-m! Why did you make us pick a fight with the Olympians? They are, like, way more powerful than we are—duh! And hello, even with our serpent legs, it was really hard to sneak up on them. We are *giants*, after all. They totally saw us coming! Let's face it— as tough as we are, we're great big mama's boys at heart. Next time we'll pick on someone our own size—if we ever get out of these volcanoes!

I'll see what I can do.

REALITY CHECK

Three-time Super Bowl champs, the New York Giants of National Football League fame take their name from the monsters of mythology. The Giants played their first game in New York City in 1925, against the Frankford Yellow Jackets.

Want to know more? Go to:
http://giants.com/

The New York Giants

The GIGANTES

"Want to play a little hardball?"

MYTH LOPEDIA

Γιγαντες

MYTHING LINK

The ancient Greeks weren't the only people who thought giants roamed the earth before humans. Giants appear in the myths and legends of many cultures around the world.

In Norse mythology of Scandinavia, the gods battled the giants just like in Greek mythology. In some European stories, giants were stupid and could easily be tricked and destroyed. And who can forget the wealthy giant in "Jack and the Beanstalk" or the giant farmer who found Gulliver in *Gulliver's Travels?*

THE BIRTH OF THE GIGANTES

Cronus comes to his mother's aid and a group of giants is born.

Gaea, the earth, had many children with Uranus, the sky. In addition to the twelve Titans, Gaea produced the three Cyclopes and the three Hecatoncheires. Uranus was so unhappy with his offspring the Cyclopes and the Hecatoncheires that he crammed each one back into the earth to prevent them from being born. In agony, Gaea begged the Titans to help destroy their father for causing her so much pain. So Cronus, the youngest Titan, attacked Uranus with a sharp **sickle**. Drops of Uranus's blood fell onto Gaea, producing the Furies, the Gigantes, and some **nymphs**.

> "Those drops of blood must have been pretty powerful to give rise to us."

Gaea

Round One

Let the games begin!

GIGANTES VS. OLYMPIANS, ROUND ONE

The Olympians crush the Titans, but they aren't out of the woods yet.

Gaea was angry. Her beloved Titans had been defeated by the upstart Olympians and were locked away deep within Tartarus. Seeking revenge, Gaea turned to her monstrously huge and savage sons, the Gigantes. These big mama's boys started piling mountains on top of mountains, coming ever closer to Mount Olympus, home of the Olympians.

The gods were frightened. Not only was their home being invaded, but the goddess Hera had foreseen that the Olympians wouldn't defeat the Gigantes without the help of a **mortal**. But who? Athena, the goddess of war, had the answer: the hero Heracles, dressed in the Nemean Lion's skin! Would Heracles be able to defeat the brutes banging on the door to Mount Olympus?

GIGANTES VS. OLYMPIANS, ROUND TWO

The Olympians have Heracles on their side: Let the battle begin!

As soon as Athena returned to Mount Olympus with Heracles, the battle began. At once the hero took aim with his bow and arrow and shot the Gigantes' leader, Alcyoneus, but the beast survived. What was going on? It turned out that Alcyoneus couldn't be killed while standing on the mountain where he had been born. Thinking fast, Heracles grabbed Alcyoneus and ran with him until they were far from the giant's birthplace. The hero's plan worked. The giant died from his wound.

"The Olympians might have been smaller but they were smarter."

GIGANTES VS. OLYMPIANS: THE FINAL ROUND

The battle rages on and the tide turns in favor of the gods.

After Alcyoneus was killed, the Gigantes started falling like bowling pins. All the Olympians and some special guest stars got in on the act. Zeus threw thunderbolts; Heracles, Apollo, and Artemis shot arrows; Hecate and Hephaestus fought with fire; and Athena hurled rocks until all 23 remaining Gigantes were destroyed and buried beneath the earth. Only one Gigante, Aristaeus, survived to tell the tale. In order to protect him from the Olympians, Gaea turned Aristaeus into a dung beetle!

REALITY CHECK

Dung beetles live all over the world, except Antarctica. They get their name from the fact that their favorite food is dung, aka animal poop. Yuck—or yum, if you're a beetle!

Want to know more? Go to: http://kids.nationalgeographic.com/Animals/CreatureFeature/Dung-beetle

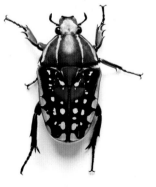
Dung beetle

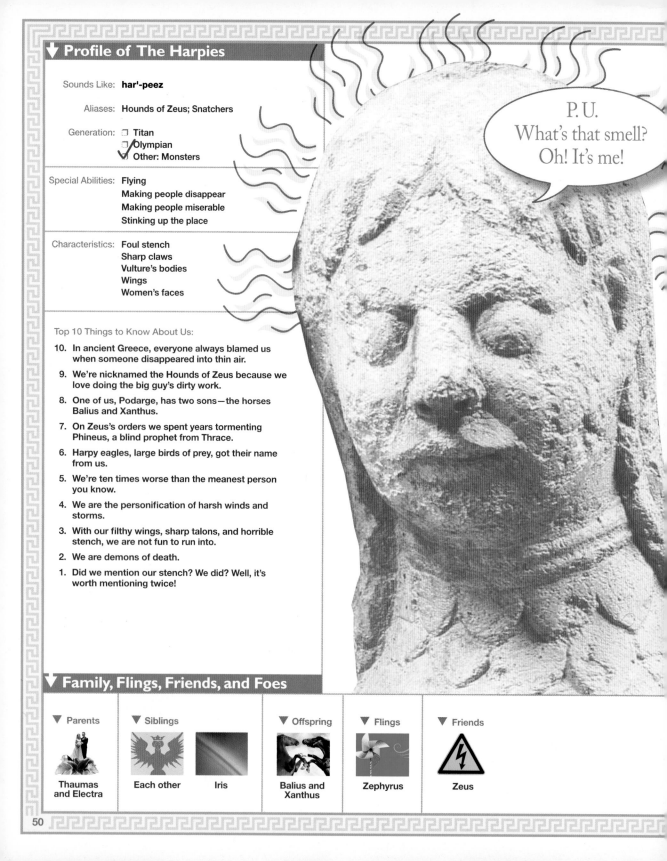

▼ Profile of The Harpies

Sounds Like: **har'-peez**

Aliases: **Hounds of Zeus; Snatchers**

Generation: ☐ Titan
☐ Olympian
☑ Other: **Monsters**

Special Abilities: **Flying**
Making people disappear
Making people miserable
Stinking up the place

Characteristics: **Foul stench**
Sharp claws
Vulture's bodies
Wings
Women's faces

> P.U.
> What's that smell?
> Oh! It's me!

Top 10 Things to Know About Us:

10. In ancient Greece, everyone always blamed us when someone disappeared into thin air.

9. We're nicknamed the Hounds of Zeus because we love doing the big guy's dirty work.

8. One of us, Podarge, has two sons—the horses Balius and Xanthus.

7. On Zeus's orders we spent years tormenting Phineus, a blind prophet from Thrace.

6. Harpy eagles, large birds of prey, got their name from us.

5. We're ten times worse than the meanest person you know.

4. We are the personification of harsh winds and storms.

3. With our filthy wings, sharp talons, and horrible stench, we are not fun to run into.

2. We are demons of death.

1. Did we mention our stench? We did? Well, it's worth mentioning twice!

▼ Family, Flings, Friends, and Foes

▼ Parents	▼ Siblings		▼ Offspring	▼ Flings	▼ Friends
Thaumas and Electra	Each other	Iris	Balius and Xanthus	Zephyrus	Zeus

The HARPIES
WHAT STINKS?

What is that *terrible* smell? Is it you? Oh, you think it's *me*? Well, thank you! You're too kind! It's just a little something I made while messing up that annoying seer Phineus's lunch. Mix a little toe jam, vomit, and rotten cheese together and voila! It's perfect for making mortals disappear—one whiff and they pass out, so they're *much* easier to carry away. Now, I've got to fly—Zeus needs me to torment someone and I can't wait! Smell you later, sweetie!

REALITY CHECK

These days, harpy eagles can be found in the rain forests of Central and South America. Like the Harpies of Greek mythology, harpy eagles are known for snatching animals for their dinner. They eat a well-balanced diet of monkeys, sloths, lizards, rodents, and other birds.

Want to know more? Go to: http://www.peregrinefund.org/explore_raptors/eagles,harpyeag.html

▼ Foes

The Argonauts

Phineus

The Boreades

It wasn't me!

51

The HARPIES

Αρπυια

"Don't make us come down there."

MYTHLOPEDIA

HERE'S LOOKING AT YOU

The Harpies were the offspring of the giant Thaumas and the sea **nymph** Electra. Also known as Snatchers and Hounds of Zeus, Harpies were monsters with the heads of women and the bodies of vultures. They were filthy, horrid, hungry creatures who tormented their prey and were demons of death. Said to number anywhere from one to five (Aello, Ocypete, Celaeno, Podarge, and Nicothoe), Harpies were **personifications** of wind and storm; they lived in the Strophades Islands in the Ionian Sea.

Eurasian black vulture

HARPING ON PHINEUS

Zeus calls out the hounds.

Phineus was one of the wisest seers, or prophets, and he didn't try to hide it. But he had a tendency to give **mortals** way too much information about the plans of the gods, making Zeus angry. To punish Phineus for being a blabbermouth, Zeus blinded him and sent the Harpies to torment him. Every time Phineus sat down to eat, the Harpies would swoop in and steal his food. What they didn't steal, they left absolutely **putrid**. Finally, Jason and the **Argonauts** stopped to ask Phineus for help locating the **Golden Fleece**. Phineus agreed to help them and in return Jason sent the Boreades, two winged youths, to chase away the Harpies.

Harpies

Phineus

Nasty!

Harpy

STORMY MEETS CALM

Podarge's offspring take after their dad.

What happens when a turbulent Harpy mates with the god of the calm west wind? Podarge, a Harpy, and Zephyrus, the warm west wind, were the parents of two special horses, Balius and Xanthus. From their mother's side, these speedy steeds inherited the ability to run like the wind. But thankfully for everyone, they also inherited their father's gentle temperament. What made them special? They could talk!

REALITY CHECK
Even today, calling someone a harpy is a serious insult. It means you think she is really irritating.

MA! What's that awful smell?

Balius and Xanthus

"Zephyrus and Podarge are like night and day but, as they say, opposites attract."

"You can run, but you can't hide."

KILL THE MESSENGERS
The Harpies are bad news.

Swooping in, snatching people up, and whisking them away were all favorite pastimes for the Harpies. And since they spent centuries scaring people half to death and taking them to Zeus knows where, the Harpies became associated with death—so much so that they were considered demons of death. Because of this association, images of Harpies were often carved onto tombs.

REALITY CHECK
Harpies were used as tomb figures. The most famous Harpy tomb comes from Lycia, in what is now southern Turkey. It's on display in London's British Museum.

Want to know more? Go to:
http://www.britishmuseum.org

Sounds Like: **heck-ah-ton-ki'-rehz**

Aliases: **Hundred Handers**
Uranids

Generation: ☐ Titan
☐ Olympian
✓ Other: Monsters

Special Abilities: **Excellent bodyguards**
Throwing one hundred things at once

Characteristics: **Fifty heads**
One hundred hands

Attributes: **Earthquakes**
Volcanoes

You're in good hands with us.

Top 10 Things to Know About Us:

10. We might look like monsters, but we're really good guys.

9. Our father, Uranus, locked us up in the depths of the earth when we were born.

8. We are very temperamental and moody.

7. Working together, we can hurl three hundred things at once.

6. Zeus was our best friend.

5. The three Cyclopes are our brothers.

4. Our mother made our father pay dearly for shoving us inside the earth.

3. After the war with the Titans, we continued to help Zeus by guarding the Titans in Tartarus.

2. The most famous of us, Briareus, is known by humans as Aegaeon.

1. We're fierce—with one hundred hands and fifty heads each. You definitely don't want to mess with us!

▼ Family, Flings, Friends, and Foes

▼ Parents	▼ Siblings						▼ Friends
Uranus and Gaea	The Cyclopes	The Titans	The Gigantes	The Furies	Typhon	Python	Zeus

The HECATONCHEIRES
YOU'RE IN GOOD HANDS

Times are tough. You want to protect your family. So let one of the Brothers Hecatoncheires lend you a hand (or a hundred!)—whatever you need, we can help! Don't be scared away by our enormous size, hundred hands, and fifty heads each; they're all at your service.

After all, fifty heads are better than one! For our A-list clientele, bodyguard services are also available. Mention coupon code HUNDRED-HANDED-ONES for 10% off our services!

▼ Foes

Uranus

The Titans

Εκατογχειρες

HERE'S LOOKING AT YOU

The Hecatoncheires were enormous beasts born with fifty heads and one hundred hands each. During the epic battle between the Titans and the Olympians, the Hecatoncheires sided with the Olympians. Their hundreds of arms and hands came in ... *ahem* ... handy for hurling rocks and boulders at the Titans.

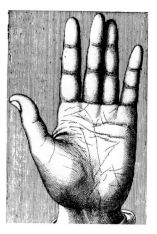

FATHER OF THE YEAR—*NOT!*

A family drama unfolds.

Most fathers jump for joy when their children are born, but not Uranus. He took one look at his sons, the Cyclopes and the Hecatoncheires, and he pushed them right back to where they came from—into Gaea, their mother and the very earth itself. This was very painful for Gaea, but nothing compared with the pain it ultimately caused Uranus! Gaea pleaded with her other children, the Titans, to punish Uranus. Cronus, the youngest Titan, carried out her wishes by attacking his father with a **sickle**. Unfortunately for the Hecatoncheires, however, Cronus wouldn't set them free. He stuck them and the Cyclopes into Tartarus, the deepest, darkest part of the **Underworld**.

All those hands creep him out!

Cronus

Being stuck inside Earth was a real downer.

HORRIFYING HELP

The Hecatoncheires pitch in.

The Cyclopes—Brontes, Steropes, and Arges—and the Hecatoncheires—Briareus, Cottus, and Gyges—were locked up inside their mother Gaea by their father Uranus. Gaea asked the Titans for help. Cronus, brother to the Cyclopes and Hecatoncheires, came to his mother's aid and defeated their father. But even though he had promised Gaea he would free his brothers, he just couldn't do it. He was afraid that one day they'd rise against him. But when the Olympians, led by Zeus, challenged the Titans, led by Cronus, to a battle that would decide the ruler of heaven and earth, Zeus made a good call: He freed the giant monsters from their Underworld prison and asked for their help defeating the Titans.

The Cyclopes and Hecatoncheires were happy to help the Olympians. The Cyclopes provided weapons: Zeus's thunderbolts, Poseidon's **trident**, and Hades' helmet of invisibility. With three hundred arms and hands among them, the Hecatoncheires could throw a lot of stuff at the Titans all at once, including giant boulders. With this kind of muscle power behind them, the Olympians defeated the Titans and sent them to Tartarus—for good! When Zeus became the most powerful god on Olympus, he continued to lean on his burly uncles for assistance. He put them to work guarding Tartarus, to make sure the Titans never escaped.

REALITY CHECK

The idea that earthquakes cause volcanoes to erupt is a myth. Earthquakes can occur near volcanoes but they are both the result of active forces within the earth. One does not cause the other.

Want to know more? Go to:
http://earthquake.usgs.gov/

Profile of Hydra

Sounds Like: **hi'-druh**

Generation:
- ☐ Titan
- ☐ Olympian
- ☑ Other: Monster

Special Abilities: Growing heads
Killing with her breath

Characteristics: One immortal head
Nine serpent heads
Poisonous blood

Top 10 Things to Know About Me:

10. In my free time, I love terrorizing the people of Lerna.

9. No one in my family will ever win a beauty contest.

8. There's a lovely little Greek island that shares my name.

7. Heracles killed me by cutting off my heads one by one and then plugging up my necks so I couldn't grow any new ones.

6. My immortal head is still squirming under a rock somewhere.

5. The smell of my tracks is enough to kill you.

4. Look for me in the sky, where you'll find a constellation named for me.

3. A tiny freshwater animal that has lots of tentacles is named hydra, after me.

2. My parents are beasts, absolute beasts!

1. I'm so monstrous, even my blood is poisonous. Just ask Heracles.

Family, Flings, Friends, and Foes

▼ **Parents**

Typhon and Echidna

▼ **Siblings**

The Nemean Lion

The Chimera

The Sphinx

Cerberus

▼ **Friends**

Hera

Carcinus

▼ **Foes**

Heracles

HYDRA
HEADS UP!

Pros of Having Nine Heads:

☞ Can have nine conversations at once— great for parties (not that I'm ever invited to parties).

☞ Losing my head is no biggie—I just grow two or three more!

☞ Nine heads = nine fabulous hairstyles!

Cons of Having Nine Heads:

☞ Nine noses means I can't get away from my own stink—P.U.!

☞ Nine mouths full of teeth = a lot of time at the dentist. Boo!

It's true—nine heads are better than one!

REALITY CHECK

Hydra lives on in a constellation best seen in the Northern Hemisphere in March and April. Of the 88 constellations recognized by the International Astrological Union, Hydra is the largest.

Want to know more? Go to: http://www.dibonsmith. com/hya_con.htm

Heracles

Hydra! Let me give those heads a trim.

59

HYDRA

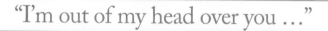

"I'm out of my head over you ..."

MYTH LOPEDIA

Υδρα

HERE'S LOOKING AT YOU

Hydra was a giant water serpent that lived in the swamps near the city of Lerna. She is most often thought of as having nine snakelike heads, although in different versions of her stories, the number ranges from five to ten thousand. Her center head was **immortal**. If another of her heads was cut off, two would grow back in its place. A whiff of her breath or her tracks was so venomous that it could destroy living beings.

"Caution: Stay far away from our family reunions."

HYDRA'S FAMILY ALBUM

The family that preys together, stays together.

Nine-headed Hydra was a member of one of the most ferocious families in town. Her parents, Typhon and Echidna, were truly unforgettable. Typhon had 101 heads and **venom** dripping from his eyes. Echidna was half-woman, half-serpent. Hydra's brothers and sisters included the three-headed watchdog Cerberus, the three-headed, fire-breathing Chimera, the enormous Nemean Lion, and the riddle-telling Sphinx that tormented the people of Thebes.

Baby Hydra

REALITY CHECK

In comics, Hydra inspired a group of evil supervillains also named Hydra. Like the monster of Greek myth, Marvel's Hydra seems unstoppable. After every defeat, the group springs back into action.

Want to know more? Go to:
http://www.marvel.com/universe/Hydra

Heracles
Hydra

HYDRA AND HERACLES
It's heads-up for a hero and a fiend.

Hydra uses her head to fight a hero.

Someone had to stop Hydra from terrorizing the people of Lerna. That person was the hero Heracles. Earlier, in a fit of madness, Heracles had killed his wife and children. As a **penance** for his crime, Heracles was assigned twelve labors by King Eurystheus. The second labor was to destroy the wretched monster.

At first, Heracles thought this labor would be a piece of cake, but every time he chopped off one of Hydra's horrible heads, two more grew back in its place!

REALITY CHECK
Hydra is not only the name of a ferocious serpent. It's also the name of a beautiful island in Greece, a constellation, and an unusual-looking freshwater animal.

Acting fast, before one of Hydra's heads could bite off his own, Heracles started chopping. But this time, when Heracles lopped off a head, he burned its **severed** neck, creating a plug so another head wouldn't grow. When only Hydra's immortal head was left, Heracles chopped it off and shoved it under a rock. Finally, the hero dipped his arrows in Hydra's poisonous blood.

Heracles's arrows dipped in Hydra's blood

HYDRA KILLS
A drop of Hydra's blood goes a long way.

While visiting Thessaly, Heracles got into a fight with a group of Centaurs. The wise Centaur Chiron got caught in the crossfire. He was struck by one of Heracles' arrows, which had been dipped in Hydra's blood. Although the wound wasn't deep, the poisonous blood caused the immortal Chiron such agony that he begged to die. Zeus agreed, and placed the beloved teacher in the heavens as a constellation.

Later, Heracles' wife, Deianeira, gave her husband a shirt that was covered with Hydra's blood. She had been told by a dying Centaur that it would strengthen Heracles' love for her. Unfortunately, when Heracles put on the poisoned shirt, it caused his skin to burn. The hero screamed in agony. Unable to remove the shirt, Heracles threw himself on a funeral **pyre**. Immortal, he rose to Mount Olympus, where he joined the gods.

HYDRA

HYDRA

HYDRA

Sounds Like: **muh-doo'-suh**

Generation: ☐ Titan
☐ ✓ Olympian
☑ Other: Monster

Special Abilities: Turning anyone who looked at her to stone

Characteristics: Claws
Lizard's scales
Snakes for hair

Let's rock!

Top 10 Things to Know About Me:

10. My sisters and I—the three Gorgons—are some of the ugliest creatures ever to roam the earth.

9. When I'm not busy terrorizing people, I like to hang out with my main man, Poseidon.

8. Athena and I never got along. She was just jealous of my powers!

7. There's a jellyfish named for me. It has a body shaped like an umbrella and tentacles that float outward.

6. My sisters Stheno and Euryale are immortal. Wish I could say the same!

5. For me, every day is a bad hair day.

4. My head might have been cut off, but it lives on ... on Athena's shield!

3. As far as I'm concerned, Perseus didn't rock.

2. My son Pegasus, a winged horse, became an inspiration for poetry. It makes a mother proud.

1. If you take one look at me, you'll be petrified ... literally!

▼ Family, Flings, Friends, and Foes

▼ Parents	▼ Siblings					▼ Offspring	
Phorcys and Ceto	Stheno	Euryale	The Graeae	Scylla	Ladon	Pegasus	Chrysaor

MEDUSA

LOOKS CAN KILL

Hello? Is this Total Monster Makeover? I need an emergency appointment. I've hit rock bottom and it shows. My hair looks like a nest of snakes. I mean, it *is* a nest of snakes, but maybe a new style would help. And my claws need a manicure. Do you do tusk-whitening? When you're done, I'd better be the most gorgeous Gorgon ever—or you'll be sorry. Now don't look at me—I don't want a stone-cold stylist!

REALITY CHECK

Medusa shares her name with a group of invertebrate marine animals known scientifically as medusae, and more commonly as jellyfish. Just as it was a good idea to avoid looking at Medusa, it's best not to touch medusae—they sting!

Want to know more? Go to: http://www.nationalgeo-graphic.com/ngkids/9608/jellyfish/

I just *had* to look!

▼ Flings

Poseidon

▼ Foes

Perseus

Athena

MEDUSA

"Just look into my eyes."

MYTHLOPEDIA

Μεδυσα

HERE'S LOOKING AT YOU

If Medusa could turn someone to stone with a glance, exactly how ugly was she? Well, for one thing, she didn't have hair. Instead, snakes sprouted and slithered out of her head. In place of skin, scales covered her body. Rather than nails, sharp bronze claws grew out of her fingers. And that's not all: She also had teeth like a boar's tusks and a tongue that hung out of her mouth.

"If you ask me, Athena was just jealous."

MEDUSA AND ATHENA

Don't mess with Athena.

It's hard to believe, but the Gorgon Medusa wasn't always hideously ugly. In fact, she was once a beautiful **mortal** maiden with a powerful boyfriend: the sea god Poseidon. So how did she go from gorgeous to grotesque? It was all thanks to the goddess Athena. Jealous of Poseidon's love for Medusa, Athena made Medusa and her sisters Stheno and Euryale so ugly that no one ever would or could look at them again!

REALITY CHECK

Many artists have tried to imagine just what Medusa looked like. One of the best-known images of Medusa was painted by the Italian artist Caravaggio around 1590. Shown below, Medusa's head has just been cut off and her face is frozen in a scream.

Want to know more? Go to:
http://www.ibiblio.org/wm/paint/auth/caravaggio/

Are those snakes on your head or are you having a really bad hair day?

MEDUSA AND PERSEUS

Perseus puts an end to Medusa's rampages.

The Gorgon Medusa had been transformed from a lovely maiden into a serpent-haired monster by the goddess Athena. One of Medusa's most terrifying qualities was the ability to turn to stone anyone who looked at her ugly mug—and let's face it, who would want to?

Meanwhile, the young mortal Perseus had been ordered by a king to retrieve the head of the Gorgon. The goddess Athena loaned Perseus her shield for protection. Holding it tight, Perseus approached Medusa's **lair** and called for her to come out. Knowing that one wrong look at Medusa would turn him to a pile of rock, the clever Perseus kept his eye on the monster's reflection in Athena's shield. As Medusa crept closer, Perseus swung his sword and beheaded her. Out of the **severed** head popped the offspring of Medusa's union with the sea god Poseidon: the winged horse Pegasus and the hero Chrysaor.

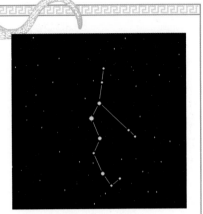

I c U, Perseus. U rock! - 4 real!- XO, Medusa

Constellation of Perseus

REALITY CHECK

You can see the hero Perseus in the constellation of the same name in the Northern Hemisphere every winter. There is even a group of stars in this constellation called Medusa's Head, because the constellation is supposed to represent the hero coming back from his victory against the Gorgon.

Want to know more? Go to:
http://www.coldwater.k12.mi.us/lms/planetarium/myth/Perseus.html

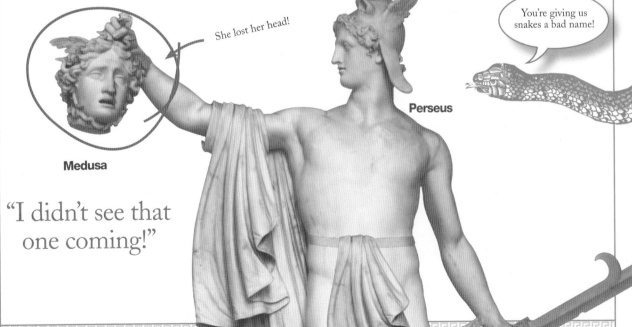

She lost her head!

Medusa

Perseus

You're giving us snakes a bad name!

"I didn't see that one coming!"

Medusa's head

Athena

MEDUSA'S DEAD HEAD

Medusa's dead head comes in handy.

After slaying Medusa, Perseus started for home, taking the Gorgon's noggin with him. When he bumped into the mighty Atlas along the way, he used Medusa's **severed** head to turn Atlas to the Atlas Mountain range. Next Perseus encountered the beautiful princess Andromeda, who was chained to a rock in the sea. Just as a sea monster was about to attack the princess, Perseus shoved Medusa's head in front of its face, turning the sea creature to stone. Perseus unchained Andromeda and the two lived happily ever after.

To thank the goddess Athena for the loan of her shield, Perseus gave her Medusa's severed head. Athena placed the face in the middle of her shield, where it would stop her enemies dead in their tracks. Medusa might have been long gone, but her power was now in the hands of the goddess.

"I liked my head better when it was on my neck!"

Perseus

The Graeae

THE GRAEAE
The Gorgons weren't the ugliest girls in town.

Deino, Enyo, and Persis, otherwise known as the Graeae, were sisters of the Gorgons and daughters of the sea god Phorcys and sea goddess Ceto. It's hard to believe, but the Graeae were even more hideous than their snake-haired sisters. They were born as old women with gray hair and wrinkles. But that's not all: These three beasties shared a grand total of one eye and one tooth among them! When Perseus was looking for Medusa, he forced the Graeae to tell him where she was by taking their eye.

REALITY CHECK
Where might you find an image of a Gorgon's head? These hideous creatures' faces were often drawn or carved on graves, temples, and shields. It was believed they would ward off evil.

Want to know more? Go to:
http://www.pantheon.org/articles/g/gorgons.html

Ewwww!

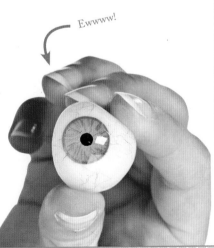

GORGONS AND GRAEAE AND M OH MY
Medusa's family has still more monsters.

The Gorgons and the Graeae were not the only monstrous offspring in Medusa's family. Her sisters also included Scylla, a sea monster who lived in a cave on one side of the straits that separate Italy and Sicily.

Scylla was a **nymph** who, like Medusa, had originally been beautiful. Glaucus, another sea god, was in love with the nymph. He asked the sorceress Circe to give Scylla a love potion. But the jealous Circe gave Scylla a poison that turned her into a monster with six heads and twelve feet.

Sailors who sailed too close to Scylla's cave would quickly fall prey to her sharp teeth. And if they veered toward the other shore, they risked being drowned by Charybdis, a monster in the form of a whirlpool.

The dragon Ladon was another member of Medusa's family. This beast, who had a hundred heads, guarded the garden of the Hesperides. He was slain by the hero Heracles, who had to retrieve golden apples from the garden as one of his twelve labors.

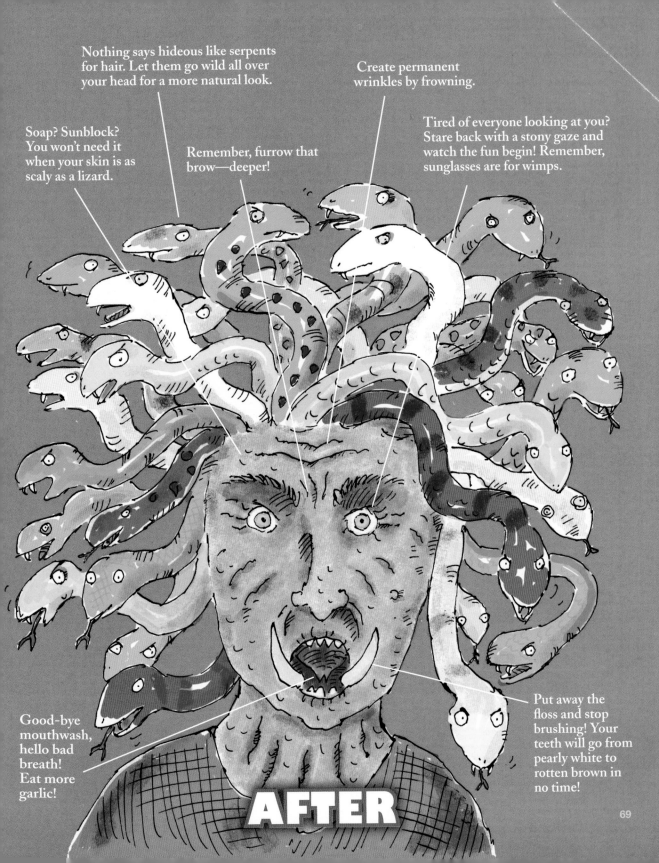

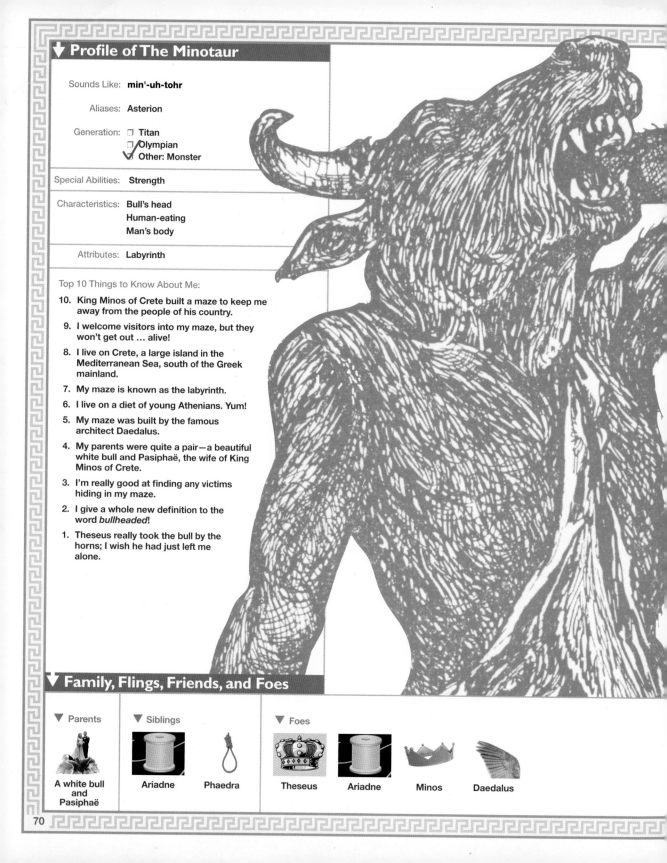

↓ Profile of The Minotaur

Sounds Like:	**min'-uh-tohr**
Aliases:	**Asterion**
Generation:	☐ Titan
	☐ Olympian
	☑ Other: Monster
Special Abilities:	**Strength**
Characteristics:	**Bull's head**
	Human-eating
	Man's body
Attributes:	**Labyrinth**

Top 10 Things to Know About Me:

10. King Minos of Crete built a maze to keep me away from the people of his country.

9. I welcome visitors into my maze, but they won't get out … alive!

8. I live on Crete, a large island in the Mediterranean Sea, south of the Greek mainland.

7. My maze is known as the labyrinth.

6. I live on a diet of young Athenians. Yum!

5. My maze was built by the famous architect Daedalus.

4. My parents were quite a pair—a beautiful white bull and Pasiphaë, the wife of King Minos of Crete.

3. I'm really good at finding any victims hiding in my maze.

2. I give a whole new definition to the word *bullheaded*!

1. Theseus really took the bull by the horns; I wish he had just left me alone.

▼ Family, Flings, Friends, and Foes

▼ Parents	▼ Siblings		▼ Foes			
A white bull and Pasiphaë	Ariadne	Phaedra	Theseus	Ariadne	Minos	Daedalus

The MINOTAUR
AN AMAZE'N VACATION

Want to get away from it all—your school, your parents, your future?

Then the Minotaur's Labyrinth Youth Resort and Spa is the place for you! With over a hundred rooms, this killer resort gives Athenian teens the chance to get lost at a destination vacation. Relax with spa treatments like the Butter Massage and the Herbed Sea Salt Scrub. You'll be aMAZEd by how much better you taste—I mean, feel. Reserve your spot today! Balls of thread must be checked at the door.

I sooooo did not sign up for this!

matador

Untitled Picasso sculpture in Chicago, Illinois

The MINOTAUR

"Stronger than a bull and twice as smart."

MYTH LOPEDIA

Μινωταυρος

HERE'S LOOKING AT YOU

The Minotaur was huge and muscular, with the head and tail of a bull on the body of a man. He was one hungry, ferocious beast!

Minotaur

THE BIRTH OF THE MINOTAUR

A king gets a gift and a god gets even.

King Minos was having trouble securing his place on the throne of Crete so he asked the gods to send him a gift to prove that he was their favorite. Poseidon came to the rescue by sending a gorgeous white bull. But things soon got crazy.

Poseidon ordered Minos to sacrifice the bull once the throne was his, but Minos tried to trick Poseidon. Instead of sacrificing the white bull, he sacrificed another one. Angry at being disobeyed, Poseidon got even by making Minos's wife, Pasiphaë, fall in love with the white bull.

In fact, Pasiphaë was so gaga over the bull that nine months later she gave birth to the Minotaur, a half-boy, half-bull. Minos imprisoned the Minotaur in a labyrinth, or maze.

Baby bull

FAST FOOD

A hero sets off to best a beast.

With his monstrous appetite, it took a lot of food to keep the Minotaur satisfied. Luckily for him, the city of Athens had earlier been defeated in a war with Crete. Following that war, Minos, the king of Crete, ruled that every year a fresh supply of 14 Athenian teenagers would be sent to Crete to be devoured by the Minotaur.

Fed up with the Minotaur's horrible appetites, the Athenian hero Theseus told his father, Aegeus, that he would go to Crete and kill the beast. Aegeus agreed to let his son go and asked him to promise one thing: If he survived his meeting with the Minotaur, he would hoist a white sail on his ship when it returned to Athens; if he died, his crew would hoist the usual black sail. With this promise, the brave Theseus joined the next group of Athenian teens as they sailed to their certain doom in Crete.

Alive   Dead

IN THE LABYRINTH

Theseus meets the monster and retraces his steps.

When Theseus arrived in Crete—along with the Minotaur's next meal—he met King Minos's daughter Ariadne. Her told her of his plan to slay the beast, and she promised to help him trick the Minotaur.

Ariadne consulted with Daedalus, the architect who had designed the labyrinth, or maze, that imprisoned the Minotaur. Daedalus gave her a ball of thread for Theseus to unwind as he made his way through the maze. Theseus would then be able to find his way out again.

On the fateful day, Theseus and the Athenians were led into the maze. As planned, Theseus wound his way through, making sure to leave a trail of thread as he went deeper and deeper into the labyrinth. Finally he came face to face with the hungry Minotaur. After a brutal fight, Theseus killed the Minotaur,

Minotaur

Theseus

gathered up the Athenians, and followed the trail of thread to freedom.

REALITY CHECK

The hedges that make up the Garden Maze at Luray Caverns in Virginia are eight feet tall and four feet wide. You can't really get lost in the maze. There are platforms to climb so you can see where you are.

Garden Maze

THESEUS AND ARIADNE

Theseus takes a trip—alone.

After Theseus killed the Minotaur, he and Ariadne certainly couldn't stay in Crete, so they fled to the nearby island of Naxos. Even though the couple seemed like a match made in heaven, Theseus and Ariadne were not meant to be together. One night while Ariadne was sleeping, Theseus left the island and headed to Athens, breaking her heart.

To punish Theseus, the goddess of love, Aphrodite, made him forget the promise he had made to his father, Aegeus: that he would hoist a white sail on his ship if he had survived his encounter with the Minotaur. Seeing a black sail on the ship as it cruised into Athens, Aegeus thought his son was dead. The heartbroken father drowned himself.

Theseus was now the king of Athens. But he wasn't the kind of ruler to just rest on his throne. He went to war with the Amazons, attempted to retrieve Persephone from the **Underworld**, and was imprisoned by Hades. At the end of his life, he was exiled from his own city—only to be thrown off a cliff and killed!

And what happened to the abandoned Ariadne? After Theseus left her, Dionysus, the fun-loving god of revelry, married her. Although she became the wife of a god—the god of entertainment and food at that—Ariadne is often associated with sorrow.

REALITY CHECK

Naxos is one of the Cyclades Islands. It is in the Aegean Sea, off the coast of Greece. Its chief town is also called Naxos.

Want to know more? Go to:
http://www.greekfestival.gr

"See Ariadne, that's what you get for working against your brother."

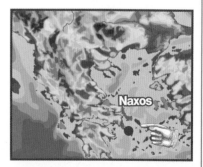

Icarus

DAEDALUS AND ICARUS

A son flies too close to the sun.

When King Minos found out that Daedalus had helped Theseus slay the Minotaur, he threw Daedalus, the architect, and his son Icarus into the labyrinth. But the **wily** and inventive Daedalus always had a trick or two up his sleeve.

Using wax and feathers, Daedalus made two sets of wings, one for himself and one for Icarus. Strapping them on, the two flew out of the labyrinth and high into the sky. Despite his father's stern warnings, Icarus flew much too high! Soon the heat of the sun melted his wax wings, and Icarus plunged into the sea below and drowned.

"Even if you escape the labyrinth, you can still get in trouble."

REALITY CHECK

Parasailing is a modern-day version of human flight. Harnessed to a canopy that is like a parachute, riders are towed by a boat that speeds up until the canopy rises into the air.

Want to know more? Go to: www.parasailing.com

MYTHING LINK

Can you find your way safely past the Minotaur and out of the maze? Follow the path with your finger.

Begin here

You're safe!

He's going down!

Icarus

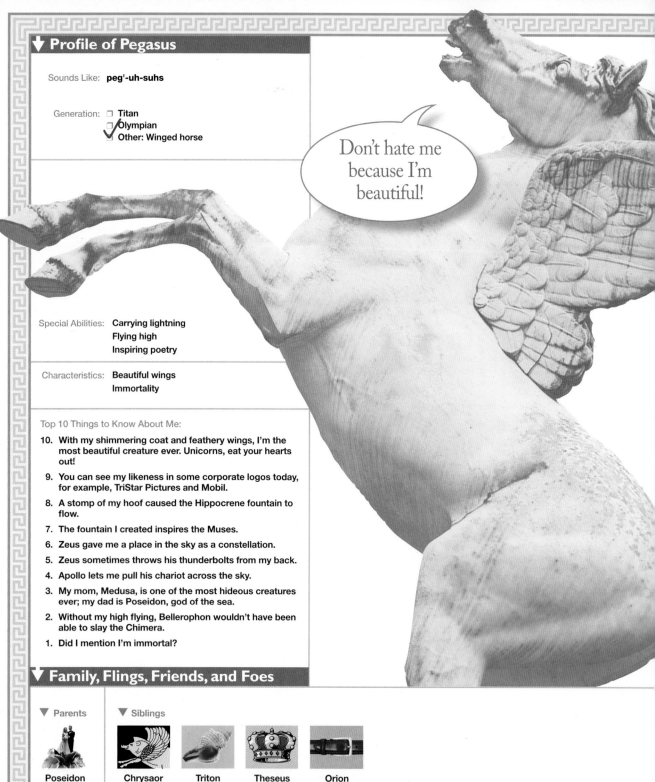

↓ Profile of Pegasus

Sounds Like: **peg'-uh-suhs**

Generation: ☐ **Titan**
☐ **Olympian**
☑ **Other: Winged horse**

Don't hate me because I'm beautiful!

Special Abilities: **Carrying lightning**
Flying high
Inspiring poetry

Characteristics: **Beautiful wings**
Immortality

Top 10 Things to Know About Me:

10. With my shimmering coat and feathery wings, I'm the most beautiful creature ever. Unicorns, eat your hearts out!

9. You can see my likeness in some corporate logos today, for example, TriStar Pictures and Mobil.

8. A stomp of my hoof caused the Hippocrene fountain to flow.

7. The fountain I created inspires the Muses.

6. Zeus gave me a place in the sky as a constellation.

5. Zeus sometimes throws his thunderbolts from my back.

4. Apollo lets me pull his chariot across the sky.

3. My mom, Medusa, is one of the most hideous creatures ever; my dad is Poseidon, god of the sea.

2. Without my high flying, Bellerophon wouldn't have been able to slay the Chimera.

1. Did I mention I'm immortal?

▼ Family, Flings, Friends, and Foes

▼ Parents

Poseidon and Medusa

▼ Siblings

Chrysaor   **Triton**   **Theseus**   **Orion**

PEGASUS
FLYING HIGH

Two Golden Horse Awards? For *me*? What an honor—for you, of course. I mean, the chance to give me *both* Most Inspiring to Poets and Most Gorgeous Horse—you must be overcome, although not surprised. Frankly the only surprise is that I wasn't nominated for Most Heroic Horse after I killed the Chimera, practically all by myself. I'd like to thank the little people—Perseus, Bellerophon, and the rest of you whose names I can't remember. Free the horses!

REALITY CHECK
You can see the image of Pegasus on many organizations' logos today, such as TriStar Pictures, Mobil, the University of Central Florida, and the Poetry Foundation, among others. Once you start looking for the winged horse, you'll see it everywhere!

Want to know more? Go to: http://www.poetry-foundation.org

A flying horse? Now I've seen everything!

unicorn

▼ Friends

Apollo

Bellerophon

Perseus

Muses

Zeus

▼ Foes

The Chimera

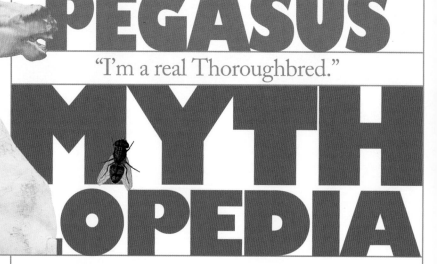

PEGASUS

"I'm a real Thoroughbred."

MYTHOPEDIA

Πεγασυς

HERE'S LOOKING AT YOU

Most horses are beautiful, with their sleek coats, strong muscles, and flowing manes and tails. But with his full, feathery wings and shining white coat, Pegasus was beyond simply beautiful—he was spectacular.

"Only one day old and already I was on an amazing adventure!"

INSPIRATION OF THE MUSES

Pegasus gets off to a quick start!

When the hero Perseus cut off the head of the monster Medusa, a beautiful creature burst forth from her **severed** neck. Talk about surprises! It was Pegasus, a full-grown, winged horse that flew off into the wild as soon as he was born. He headed for Mount Helicon, in Corinth, where he stamped his hoof so hard one day that a fountain sprang out of the earth. This fountain, called the Hippocrene, became an inspiration to the Muses, who were the goddesses of the arts, and the winged Pegasus became their symbol.

REALITY CHECK

Named in honor of Pegasus, the Hippocrene stills exists on Mount Helicon in central Greece. Its name comes from the Greek *hippos*, "horse," and *krene*, "fountain."

Want to know more? Go to:
http://www.loggia.com/myth/helicon.html

Pegasus

Medusa

PEGASUS AND BELLEROPHON

Pegasus stops for a sip and gets roped into a visit.

One day, as Pegasus stood beside a pond drinking water, the Corinthian hero Bellerophon stepped up beside him. On a mission to slay the Chimera, a fierce monster, Bellerophon had a magical golden **bridle** that had been given to him by the goddess Athena. He threw the bridle on Pegasus and jumped astride the horse. With barely a "giddyap," off they flew.

After killing the Chimera, Bellerophon became a bit too confident. He decided to ride Pegasus to Olympus to visit the gods. But the mighty Zeus would have none of that! To stop the boastful intruder, Zeus sent a fly to sting Pegasus. The painful sting caused Pegasus to buck and kick, and Bellerophon flew off the horse and crashed to Earth. The hero spent the rest of his days wandering in confusion. As for Pegasus, he continued on to Olympus, where he became the pampered horse of the gods.

Zeus sent me!

Bellerophon

The Chimera

Pegasus

> "Every Greek hero wanted to ride me to visit the gods."

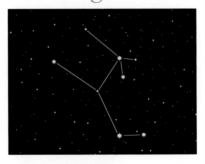

REALITY CHECK

To see Pegasus today, just look up. The constellation Pegasus is visible in the autumn sky to observers in the Northern Hemisphere. Its most visible configuration of stars is the Great Square of Pegasus— four bright stars that form the body of the horse.

Want to know more? Go to:
*http://www.windows.ucar.edu/tour/link/=/the_*
universe/Constellations/pegasus.html&edu=high

WINGED HEROES

Flying creatures come to the rescue.

Pegasus wasn't the only hero with wings. The Boreades, sons of the North Wind, were winged youths who traveled with the **Argonauts**, the adventurers who helped Jason capture the **Golden Fleece**. They are most famous for chasing the Harpies away from the prophet Phineus who'd told mortals the secrets of the gods.

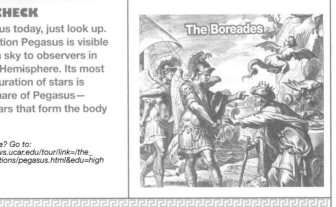

The Boreades

▼ Profile of Prophets and Oracles

Today's your lucky day!

Your future looks bright.

Sounds Like: kal'-kuhs (Calchas)
oar'-uh-kuhl at dell'-fie (Oracle at Delphi)
fin'-i-uhs (Phineus)
ty-ree'-see-uhs (Tresias)

Generation: ☐ Titan
☐ Olympian
☑ Other: Seer

Calchas, Special Abilities:	Best seer in ancient Greece
Oracle at Delphi, Special Abilities:	Speaking the word of Apollo
Attributes:	Bronze stool
	Laurel leaves
	Vapors
Phineus, Special Abilities:	Seeing what only the gods knew
Tiresias, Special Abilities:	Seeing the future
	Understanding the language of birds
Characteristics:	Blindness
Attributes:	Gold staff

Top 10 Things to Know About Us:

10. It's me, Tiresias. I work for King Oedipus.

9. Odysseus came to the Underworld to consult with my spirit.

8. Take my advice: If you glimpse a goddess in her bathtub, it's best to look the other way!

7. Phineus here. I'm so glad to be rid of those Harpies. Thanks, Jason!

6. Sometimes the gods get mad at us for blabbing their secrets—just ask me.

5. My turn, guys. I, Calchas, went to the Trojan War with Agamemnon. What a scene!

4. It was downhill from there. I died when another prophet got the best of me.

3. Oracle at Delphi speaking. Ask me anything—I'm the original help desk.

2. Just to complicate life, I'm a person, a place, and a thing. You'd better hope I never show up on a vocabulary quiz.

1. Where do I hang out? The center of the universe!

▼ Family, Flings, Friends, and Foes

Parents

▼ Calchas ▼ Phineus ▼ Tiresias

Thestor and Megara Agenor Everes and Chariclo

Siblings

▼ Phineus

Europa Cadmus

Friends

▼ Phineus

The Argonauts The Boreades

PROPHETS AND ORACLES
WE KNOW IT ALL!

Brring! Thanks for calling House of Prophets, Tiresias speaking. Hi, Odysseus; I'll transfer you to Calchas—he's expecting your call. The Trojan War will work out fine. Promise! *Brrring*! House of Prophets, Tiresias here. Sorry, Phineus is on leave to deal with those Harpies. Please hold for the next available seer. *Brring*! House of Prophets, this is Tiresias. You called for Apollo? Please hold for the Pythia; she's handling his calls. *Brring*! Zeus! I *knew* it was you! Settle a debate between you and Hera? I don't see why not. Come on down!

A temple at Delphi

▼ Tiresias

Oedipus

Odysseus

Zeus

Foes

▼ Calchas ▼ Phineus ▼ Tiresias

Mopus

The Harpies

Athena

Hera

81

Προφητης

HERE'S LOOKING AT YOU

Prophets aren't the only ones who predict the future.

So do:

➤ clairvoyants
➤ fortune tellers
➤ psychics
➤ seers
➤ soothsayers
➤ weather forecasters

Fortune Teller

CALCHAS SEES THE WAY TO VICTORY

A prophet shares a great idea for a present.

The great seer, or prophet, Calchas accompanied Agamemnon, a Greek general, during the Trojan War. Through his **prophecies**, Calchas helped the Greeks win the war. In fact it was Calchas who communicated to the hero Odysseus Athena's brilliant idea of presenting a wooden horse (secretly filled with Greek soldiers) as a "gift" to the Trojans. But even a great prophet can feel like a failure sometimes. After the war, Calchas and a seer named Mopus had a contest to see who could correctly guess the number of figs on a tree. Calchas lost not only the contest, but also his will to live.

Calchas

Harpy

PHINEUS AND THE HARPIES
One good turn deserves another!

To punish Phineus for revealing the plans of the gods to **mortals**, Zeus sent the Harpies to torment the blabbermouth seer. Every time Phineus sat down to eat, the hideous Harpies would swoop in and steal or defile his food.

In the meantime, Jason and his crew of **Argonauts** were sailing in search of the **Golden Fleece**. Along the way they met the suffering Phineus. Phineus told the sailors about his troubles and promised to help them find the Golden Fleece if they'd help him get rid of the Harpies. Jason agreed. When the Harpies arrived at mealtime, the Argonauts sent two winged youths, the Boreades, after the demons. In return, Phineus used his power of prophecy to recommend the best route for the next leg of the Argonauts' journey.

THE ORACLE AT DELPHI
Any questions? Ask the Oracle at Delphi.

Apollo, the god of prophecy, found the perfect spot for his temple and **oracle**. Perfect except for one annoying problem: An enormous and very nasty serpent, Python, lived on Mount Parnassus, right where Apollo's temple was to be built. Before the god could build his temple, he had to slay Python. Once the serpent was out of the way, Apollo set up his oracle in the temple. There, a priestess called the Pythia sat on a tripod, or three-legged stool, and took questions from mortals, ranging from the best time to plant crops to when to declare war. Apollo would answer through the Pythia, and priests would interpret the answers.

The world's first help desk!

Oracle at Delphi

TIRESIAS LOSES HIS SIGHT
A seer gets stuck in the middle of a domestic dispute.

Tiresias had an interesting past: He had spent time as a man and as a woman! So, in the midst of a disagreement about whether men or women enjoyed being in love more, the great god Zeus and his wife, Hera, decided to consult someone who would surely know the answer: Tiresias. When he answered "women," Hera lost her cool. As the unhappy wife of a famous ladies' man, the goddess was certain that men had more fun in the love department. In a fit of rage, Hera blinded the helpless seer. Zeus, who happened to agree with Tiresias, felt awful about his wife's actions, so he gave Tiresias the gift of prophecy. Why didn't the almighty Zeus simply return Tiresias's sight? He couldn't! A god or goddess couldn't undo a gift or curse bestowed by another of their **immortal** clan.

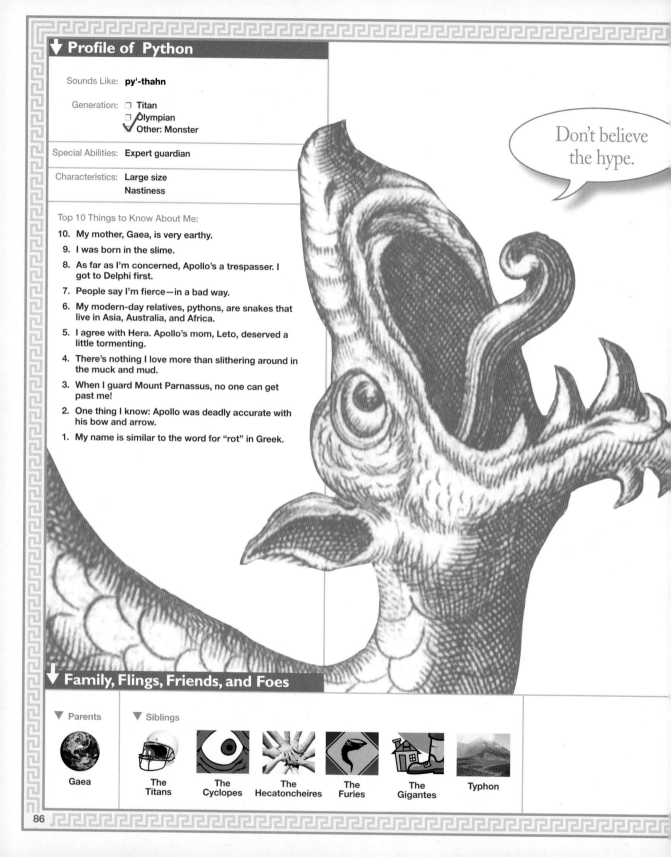

▼ Profile of Python

Sounds Like:	**py'-thahn**
Generation:	☐ Titan ☐ Olympian ☑ Other: Monster
Special Abilities:	**Expert guardian**
Characteristics:	**Large size** **Nastiness**

Top 10 Things to Know About Me:

10. My mother, Gaea, is very earthy.

9. I was born in the slime.

8. As far as I'm concerned, Apollo's a trespasser. I got to Delphi first.

7. People say I'm fierce—in a bad way.

6. My modern-day relatives, pythons, are snakes that live in Asia, Australia, and Africa.

5. I agree with Hera. Apollo's mom, Leto, deserved a little tormenting.

4. There's nothing I love more than slithering around in the muck and mud.

3. When I guard Mount Parnassus, no one can get past me!

2. One thing I know: Apollo was deadly accurate with his bow and arrow.

1. My name is similar to the word for "rot" in Greek.

Don't believe the hype.

▼ Family, Flings, Friends, and Foes

▼ Parents	▼ Siblings					
Gaea	The Titans	The Cyclopes	The Hecatoncheires	The Furies	The Gigantes	Typhon

PYTHON
My Sssside of the Sssstory

Ssssscandal! I wassss minding my own businessss, ssssunning myself at Delphi, when ssssneaky Apollo sssslayed me in cold blood! And what wassss hissss excusssse? That I sssstalked his mom? That'ssss sssslander! Besidessss, sssshe had it coming—jusssst asssssk Hera. Sssserioussssly, I sssssusssspect Apollo wanted my mountain for himssssself. What wassss the sssso-called god of prophecy without hissss own oracle? Two wordssss: A sssssham! If you ssssee him, tell him I hope he rotssss! Sssssnap!

REALITY CHECK

Real-life pythons are almost as frightening as their mythic ancestor. They kill prey by wrapping themselves around it and squeezing so tightly that the captured prey can't breathe. These humongous snakes are native to Asia, Australia, and Africa. The largest one ever measured was 28 feet long!

Want to know more? Go to: http:// www.sandiegozoo. org/animalbytes/t-python. html

▼ **Friends**

Hera

▼ **Foes**

Apollo

That's a big snake!

Apollo

PYTHON

"I wassss here firsssst."

MYTH LOPEDIA

Πψθον

HERE'S LOOKING AT YOU

What an image! Smelly, slimy, huge, and territorial—where does a beast like that come from? In Greek myth, there was a great flood that covered Gaea, the earth, in water. As the water evaporated, rotting muck was left behind. Python, a huge serpent, was born from this slimy filth.

PYTHON MEETS APOLLO

Python plays keep away with Apollo, and loses.

There are several stories about why the god Apollo slayed Python. In one, Apollo is out for revenge because the jealous goddess Hera enlisted Python's help in tormenting Apollo's mom, Leto, when she was ready to give birth to Apollo and Artemis. In another, Apollo slays Python so he can establish his **oracle** on Mount Parnassus, where Python lives. In a different twist, Apollo must kill the beast because she was terrorizing the people on Mount Parnassus.

Apollo

Python

But no matter the details, the outcome is always the same. Apollo slays Python with his bow and arrow and sets up shop on Mount Parnassus.

"I was born bad and ready for a fight."

PYTHON ROTS

A rotting serpent lends her name to a sacred place.

Apollo, the god of **prophecy**, established his temple on Mount Parnassus—once Python was out of the way. Meanwhile, the dead Python rotted away on the mountainside. The decaying serpent inspired the location's name, Pytho (it was later called Delphi), and Apollo's epithet, or nickname, Pythian, both of which resemble the Greek word for "rot." Finally, Apollo's oracle, who communicated his prophecies to **mortals**, was known as the Pythia.

> "Apollo was treated like a hero and I was dead. Doesn't sound fair to me."

Apollo
Python

Painting Drama Poetry

FUN AND GAMES

Everyone celebrates after Apollo's victory.

The Pythian Games, held every four years, **commemorated** Apollo's victory over Python. The first games were held in 582 BCE. Like today's Olympic Games, the Pythian Games were athletic contests, but in honor of Apollo, the god of music and poetry, the games also featured artistic contests. In the fourth century CE, the games were abandoned. Fast forward to the year 2000: The first Delphic Games, the new version of the Pythian Games, were held in Moscow, Russia. As in the Olympic Games, countries from all over the world sent participants. But, unlike the Olympics, these games featured artistic competitions rather than athletic ones.

Malaysia

REALITY CHECK

The second Delphic Games took place in 2005 in Malaysia. Delphic Games are scheduled for 2009 in South Korea.

Want to know more? Go to: http://www.delphic.org/index.php?id=392&L=1

> "Everyone had fun celebrating my death. How rude!"

Profile of The Satyrs

Sounds Like: say'-turz

Generation:
- ☐ Titan
- ☐ Olympian
- ☑ Other: Woodland creatures

Special Abilities: Dancing
Playing reed instruments
Prophecy

Characteristics: Faces and upper bodies of a man
Goat's horns
Goat's legs
Horse's tail
Pointed ears

Top 10 Things to Know About Us:

10. As Dionysus's attendants, we go to all the best parties.

9. We love flirting with nymphs.

8. We star in satyr plays, short comedies staged to cheer up the audience after they've watched a Greek tragedy.

7. We like the good things in life—food, music, and dance.

6. Although we have a reputation for being lazy, we are actually great musicians.

5. Ever hear the word *panic*? That comes from our buddy Pan.

4. If there's action, we're there. They should make a reality show about us!

3. The most famous of us, Silenus, can predict the future.

2. One of our pals, Marsyas, challenged Apollo to a music contest and lost!

1. We're half beast, half man—and a whole lotta fun.

Let's party!

Family, Flings, Friends, and Foes

▼ Parents	▼ Siblings	▼ Flings	▼ Friends	▼ Foes	
Hermes and Iphthime	Pan	Woodland nymphs	Dionysus	Midas	Apollo

The SATYRS

PARTY ANIMALS

YO YO YO YO! Got to get my party on, bros! I'm packin' my panpipes and my tambourine and I'm hoping for a dance-off with a nymph. Is Dionysus in the house? That dude knows how to bring the party. Just don't horn in on his turf or act like a horse's behind. So what are we waiting for? Let's hoof it into the woods for some wild times. I predict this party is gonna rock!

REALITY CHECK

A type of tropical forest-dwelling butterfly, commonly known as satyr, takes its name from the fun-loving creatures of myth. The scientific name for satyr butterflies is *Euptychia hermes*. To confuse predators, their wings have markings that look like eyes.

Want to know more? Go to:
http://www.insects.org/
entophiles/lepidoptera/
lepi_023.html

He looks cute in that hat.

nymphs

You said it, sister!

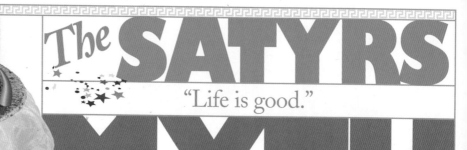

The SATYRS

"Life is good."

MYTHLOPEDIA

Σατψροι

HERE'S LOOKING AT YOU

What did satyrs look like? You'd think that as the life of every party they'd be the best-looking creatures around. Not so. These beasts were half-man, half-goat. They had the upper torso of a human but with horns on their heads and pointed ears. The rest of their body was that of a goat, including four furry legs and a tail. But that sure didn't stop them from having fun and being the center of attention.

"Even satyrs know that too much of a good thing isn't good for anyone."

SILENUS AND KING MIDAS

A host with the most gets a gift from a guest.

The satyr Silenus paid a visit to King Midas of Phrygia. A generous host, Midas welcomed Silenus with open arms, putting him up and entertaining him for five days. When the god Dionysus arrived to take Silenus back home, he granted Midas one wish as a reward for his hospitality. Midas asked that from that day forward everything he touched would turn to gold. Dionysus granted the wish, but the results were disastrous. Midas's food and water turned to gold so he couldn't eat or drink, and he even turned his daughter into gold! Midas regretted his wish and asked to be released from it. He was allowed to wash his hands in the Pactolus River. Midas lost the gift of the golden touch, but the sands of the river turned gold!

Golden meal!

MUSICAL THROWDOWN

Apollo: 1, Marsyas: 0

King Midas insisted that the satyr Marsyas was a better musician than the god Apollo, so the satyr challenged the god to a contest. Whoever won could do what he wished with the loser. Apollo strummed his **lyre** like a god, first playing it right side up, then upside down.

Poor Marsyas tooted his flute but he was no match for Apollo. What was the losing satyr's fate? Apollo hung him from a tree and skinned him alive! But that's not all. To teach the king a lesson about doubting the skills of a god, Apollo gave Midas the ears of a donkey. The king concealed the ears under a **turban**, permitting no one but his barber to see them. The barber, sworn to silence, whispered the secret into a hole in the ground and then filled it with dirt. Reeds soon grew over the hole. When the wind blew, the reeds could be heard whispering Midas's secret.

> "We were symbols for nature's plenty— and we definitely had plenty of fun!"

Dionysus

MYTHING LINK

Dionysus was the god of fertility, ritual dance, and mysticism. He also supposedly invented winemaking and was considered the patron of poetry, song, and drama. The ancient Greeks devoted entire months to throwing parties in his honor. The satyrs had it right—he was the god to have fun with!

Satyr

REALITY CHECK

In ancient Greece, satyr plays were brief comedies presented after a tragic play at the festivals honoring the god Dionysus. Their style was crude, with the chorus dressed in animal skins and tails to represent satyrs. The only complete satyr play known today is Euripides' *Cyclops*.

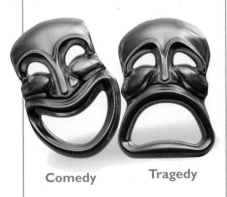
Comedy   Tragedy

▼ Profile of The Sirens

Sounds Like: **sie'-renz**

Generation:
- ☐ Titan
- ☑ Olympian
- ☑ Other: Bird women

Special Abilities: Power of persuasion
Singing

Characteristics: Birds' bodies
Birds' wings
Women's heads

Top 10 Things to Know About Us:

10. We look a bit like birds and sing like them too!

9. Don't confuse our song with police, fire, or ambulance sirens.

8. Only one mortal heard our song and lived to tell the tale: Odysseus.

7. When we die, we become rocks in the sea.

6. The German Lorelei is a lot like us.

5. Our song is sweeter than anything you can imagine.

4. We live on an island in the sea.

3. The Starbucks coffee logo features an image of one of us.

2. We think it was rude that Orpheus tried to drown us out.

1. We're sorry about all the shipwrecks! NOT!

♪ Did you ever know that you're ♪ our hero ...

▼ Family, Flings, Friends, and Foes

▼ Parents	▼ Siblings	▼ Foes			
Achelous and Melpomene	Each other	Orpheus	Jason	The Argonauts	Odysseus

The SIRENS

HEY SAILOR, OVER HERE!

Row, row, row your boat
Right into our trap.
Listen to our pretty song
And throw away your map.
Row, row, row this way
Don't plug up your ears.
We'll sing louder if you do
So everyone can hear.
Row, row, row your boat
Crash it on the shore.
Screams abound as sailors drown
on the ocean floor!

REALITY CHECK

If you're looking for a siren today, you may come across a type of salamander that lives in the southeastern United States. The largest of these salamanders, called the great siren or *Siren lacertina*, can grow up to three feet long!

Where's that music coming from?

The SIRENS

"We're hotter than a steaming cup of coffee."

MYTH LOPEDIA

Σιρεν

HERE'S LOOKING AT YOU

It's fitting that the Sirens are described as having the bodies of birds, since their song was said to be just as lovely as a bird's. Ancient Greek writers called them clear-voiced with honey-tongued throats. With voices like that, it's easy to understand why sailors found it so difficult to pass them by.

And it wasn't just how they sang, but also their tempting words:

"No one ever sailed past us without staying to hear the enchanting sweetness of our song—and he who listens will go on his way not only charmed, but wiser, for we ... can tell you everything that is going to happen over the whole world."
—Homer, *The Odyssey*, Book XII

THE SIRENS AND ODYSSEUS

Odysseus hears the Sirens' song but sails on.

At the end of the Trojan War, it took the hero Odysseus ten years to sail home to Ithaca. Along the way, Odysseus and his crew encountered one **obstacle** after another—from sorceresses to monsters. But the singing Sirens proved to be one of the greatest challenges of all. These sea **nymphs** sang melodies so beautiful that sailors passing their rocky island were lured to shipwreck and death. As Odysseus's ship drew near their island, he ordered his men to plug their ears with beeswax so that they couldn't hear the Sirens' songs, and to tie him to the ship's mast so that he could listen but couldn't swim ashore. Odysseus became one of the few **mortals** who lived to tell the tale of the Sirens' song.

REALITY CHECK

The Odyssey is a Greek epic poem in 24 books by Homer. It tells the story of the ten-year journey home of Odysseus after the Trojan War.

Beat the Sirens at their own game.

Orpheus

REALITY CHECK
Take a look at the creature on the Starbucks logo. It's a Siren with a mermaid's tail. Starbucks chose this figure for its logo to represent the irresistibility of its coffee.

Siren

THE SIRENS AND THE ARGONAUTS

Orpheus outplays the Sirens and they turn to rock.

On their quest to capture the **Golden Fleece**, Jason and his crew of Argonauts sailed past the Sirens' rock. The Sirens, a group of singing bird-women, were delighted to have a captive audience and they began to sing their lovely, haunting song. Fortunately Orpheus, the great Greek musician, was onboard. When he heard the Sirens singing, he drowned them out by playing his **lyre**. Orpheus's music was even more beautiful than the Sirens' voices. Defeated, the unhappy bird-women jumped into the sea and turned into rocks.

REALITY CHECK

In her poem "Siren Song," Margaret Atwood writes of "the song that is irresistible."

Want to read the entire poem? Go to: http://www.poetryfoundation.org/archive/poem.html?id=21988

"Orpheus played such a pretty song on his lyre it broke our hearts."

MYTHING LINK

In German folklore, a maiden named Lorelei jumped into the Rhine River when she found out her honey loved somebody else. Lorelei's spirit sang a beautiful song that tempted sailors to veer off course and head for certain doom. Sound familiar?

Rhine River

▼ Profile of The Sphinx

Sounds Like: **sfinks**

Generation:
- ☐ Titan
- ☐ Olympian
- ☑ Other: Monster

Special Abilities: **Bringing bad luck**
Telling riddles

Characteristics: **Eagle's wings**
Human-eater
Lion's body
Serpent's tail
Woman's head

Top 10 Things to Know About Me:

10. You might recognize my name from my more famous Egyptian cousin, the Great Sphinx at Giza.

9. Oedipus solved my riddle and became king of Thebes.

8. I'm four creatures in one—a lion, a human female, an eagle, and a serpent.

7. My name comes from the Greek word meaning "to strangle."

6. There's a type of moth named after me.

5. In ancient Greece you would often find my image at the entrance to a temple, making sure everything was safe and sound.

4. The gods sent me to Thebes to punish the people there.

3. These days if you call someone by my name it means he or she is very mysterious.

2. The Muses taught me my riddle.

1. Can you answer my riddle? What is it that walks on four legs in the morning, on two legs at noon, and on three legs in the evening?

Answer: A human being. It crawls on all fours as a baby, walks upright on two legs as an adult, then walks with the help of a cane in old age.

Wrong answer!

▼ Family, Flings, Friends, and Foes

▼ Parents	▼ Siblings				▼ Friends	▼ Foes
Typhon and Echidna	The Nemean Lion	Cerberus	The Chimera	Hydra	Hera	Oedipus

The SPHINX

RIDDLE ME THIS

Stop me if you've heard this one—and guess carefully, because if you're wrong, you're on the menu! What has a woman's head, a lion's body, a serpent's tail, and an eagle's wings? Oh—you guessed me? Well, yeah, technically, that's correct. But that one was easy! How about *this*: What loves to eat humans, tell riddles, and bring bad luck? Oh. Yeah, me again. Good guess, buddy. Okay, here's one that will stump you. What am I having for lunch? *YOU!*

REALITY CHECK

The oldest, most famous Egyptian sphinx is the Great Sphinx at Giza, dating from the twenty-sixth century BCE. It is a huge sculpture carved from a natural bluff of rock. The body has the shape of a reclining lion, and its head is that of a king wearing the royal headdress. The figure looks east toward the Nile Valley.

Want to know more? Go to: http://www.guardians.net/ egypt/sphinx/

> I should have done my homework.

Oedipus

99

The SPHINX

"Keep them guessing. That's my motto!"

MYTHLOPEDIA

Σφινξ

HERE'S LOOKING AT YOU

A gathering of the Sphinx's family would be a horrifying sight. Her father, Typhon, was a multiheaded giant with serpents in place of his legs. Her mother, Echidna, had the head of a beautiful **nymph**, but her beauty ended there—her body was that of a serpent. And her brothers and sisters? They included the ferocious Nemean Lion; Cerberus, a three-headed dog; the Chimera, a beast that combined parts of a lion, a goat, and a serpent; and Hydra, a nine-headed serpent. It's hard to imagine a group more frightening!

The Sphinx

Oedipus

THE RIDDLE OF THE SPHINX

A monster terrorizes a city with a bad joke.

The city of Thebes was under siege by the Sphinx, a monster with the body of a reclining lion and the chest and face of a woman. This creature, a demon of death and bad luck, had been sent by the gods to punish the people of Thebes. Perched on a rock outside the gates to the city, the Sphinx terrorized anyone who passed by with the following riddle: "What is it that walks on four legs in the morning, on two legs at noon, and on three legs in the evening?" When they failed to guess correctly—and so far everybody had failed—

the Sphinx gobbled them up!

The king of Thebes promised that anyone who correctly answered the riddle would succeed him as king. One day the hero Oedipus wandered by on his way home from a visit to the **Oracle** at Delphi. He stopped before the Sphinx as she posed her riddle. The hero thought for a moment, then answered: "A human being. It crawls on all fours as a baby, walks upright on two legs as an adult, then walks with the help of a cane in old age." Oedipus was correct, and the Sphinx was furious. In a rage, the beast hurled herself from her perch and died. As for Oedipus, he became king of Thebes. But that's not the whole story.

THE STORY OF OEDIPUS

A little baby has bad luck.

Oedipus had been born to King Laius and Queen Jocasta of Thebes. When Oedipus was born, the Oracle at Delphi told Laius and Jocasta that one day their son would kill his father and marry his mother. The king and queen were horrified. To prevent the **prophecy** from coming true, they gave their baby to a shepherd and told him to leave the child in a pasture to die. The baby's feet had been pierced and tied together (the name Oedipus means "swollen feet"). But instead of leaving the baby to die, the shepherd gave him to a man who was traveling to the city of Corinth. There Oedipus was adopted by King Polybus and Queen Periboea.

The Sphinx

Oedipus

OEDIPUS: FROM BAD TO WORSE

There's no news like bad news.

When he was grown, Oedipus heard a rumor that he was not really Polybus's son. He went to Delphi to learn the truth. The Oracle at Delphi did not answer his question but instead prophesied that Oedipus would kill his father and marry his mother. Thinking the prophecy referred to King Polybus and Queen Periboea, Oedipus decided not to return to Corinth. On his way out of Delphi, Oedipus was forced off the road by a man traveling with four attendants. Although Oedipus didn't recognize him, the man was none other than King Laius of Thebes. Furious, Oedipus killed Laius and three of the attendants. The fourth escaped to report the king's death to the people of Thebes. Oedipus continued to Thebes, where he encountered the Sphinx outside the gates and correctly answered her riddle. Hailed as a hero when he arrived in the city, Oedipus was offered the throne as well as the hand in marriage of the widowed queen, Jocasta. In time, Oedipus and Jocasta had two sons and two daughters. They were blissfully happy, for a while.

... AND WORSE

More bad news unfolds.

Thebes was stricken by a plague. The people begged Oedipus for a solution. So he sent his brother-in-law Creon to Delphi to plead for the god Apollo's help. Apollo's oracle declared that the plague would go away when Laius's murderer was punished. When Oedipus consulted with the prophet Tiresias to find out the identity of the murderer, Tiresias revealed that it was Oedipus. Then he told Oedipus everything: That his mother had left him with a shepherd because of a prophecy that he'd kill his father and marry his mother; that he'd been adopted by King Polybus; and that his wife, Jocasta, was really his mother. Horrified, Oedipus realized it was all true. He rushed into the palace, where he found that Jocasta had hanged herself. Insane with shame and grief, Oedipus blinded himself. Creon took the throne and Oedipus was banished from Thebes. Oedipus later died near Athens.

MYTHING LINK

The Oracle at Delphi was located in the temple of Apollo, the god of prophecy. **Mortals** would go to the temple to consult with the god through the oracle. Even politicians consulted the oracle before making important decisions.

Welcome to
MS. SPHINX'S CLASS!

Ms. Sphinx is one tough teacher. Let's just say there are no make-up quizzes in her classroom.

DUNCE

What goes on four legs in the morning, on two legs at noon, and on three legs in the evening?

Profile of Triton

Sounds Like: try'-ton

Generation:
- ☐ Titan
- ☐ Olympian
- ☑ Other: Sea god

Special Abilities: Announcing Poseidon's entrances
Controlling the ocean

Characteristics: Fish tail

Attributes: Conch shell
Trident

Top 10 Things to Know About Me:

10. It doesn't get much better than where I live—in a golden palace under the sea.

9. I'm still hanging out with my father, Poseidon, as the largest of his moons!

8. One blow on my conch-shell trumpet and I can really make waves.

7. I once drowned a man who challenged me to a trumpeting contest.

6. I go everywhere with my entourage of sea nymphs and tritons.

5. I'm not all bad—I guided my fair share of sailors who were lost at sea.

4. I guided the Argonauts back on course.

3. My uncle is Zeus, king of the gods.

2. Wherever my father goes, I sound my trumpet to let everyone knows he's arrived.

1. I'm half-man, half-fish but all attitude.

Gnarly, dude!

Family, Flings, Friends, and Foes

▼ Parents

Poseidon and Amphitrite

▼ Siblings

Pegasus

Chrysaor

Theseus

Orion

▼ Offspring

Pallas

Calliste

Triteia

TRITON

DO YOU KNOW WHO MY FATHER IS?

Excuse me? What do you mean, I'm not on the list? Do you know who my father is? Here's a hint: god of the sea, Zeus's big brother, swims softly and carries a big trident. Ring any bells? That's right, Poseidon is my pops, and I always announce his arrival. Do you think I carry around this conch shell for my health? Where Dad goes, I go first. Now get out of my way before I turn you into fish sticks!

REALITY CHECK

The eighth planet in our solar system is named for Triton's father, Poseidon, the god of the sea (his Roman name is Neptune). And what's the name of Neptune's largest moon? Triton!

Want to know more? Go to: http://solarsystem. nasa.gov/planets/profile. cfm?Object=Nep_Triton

Hang ten!

▼ Friends

Tritons

Aeneas

The Argonauts

Sea nymphs

Hippocamps

▼ Foes

Misenus

TRITON

"Surf's up!"

MYTHLOPEDIA

Τριτων

HERE'S LOOKING AT YOU

Triton was built for a life at sea. With a human torso, the tail of a fish, and rock-hard muscles, this merman could swim faster than any mere mortal. Triton always carried his conch-shell trumpet and **trident** so he could control the seas no matter where he was.

Triton helped them out of a tough spot!

TRITON AND THE ARGONAUTS

A hero blows off course and the prince of the sea comes to the rescue.

On his quest to obtain the **Golden Fleece**, a treasured golden sheepskin, Jason and the **Argonauts**, the crew onboard the *Argo*, faced many challenges. One of the greatest challenges occurred when a gust of wind blew the *Argo* into the shallow waters of Lake Tritonis in Libya. Jason and his crew would have been stranded there forever if the prince of the sea, Triton, hadn't guided them safely through a narrow channel and back into the open sea.

REALITY CHECK

Triton might look familiar to you if you've seen the movie *The Little Mermaid*. Ariel's father was a merman and king of the sea, and his name was King Triton!

Argonauts

TRITON'S TEMPER

Triton is put to the test—and comes out on top!

After Troy fell and the Trojan War ended, Aeneas, who had been a Trojan prince, set off with a crew for Italy to escape the Greeks. Like many journeys at sea, his trip was difficult. At one point, Aeneas's ship ran aground or, in landlubber terms, became stuck on land. Triton, the prince of the sea, came eagerly to the rescue.

Among Aeneas's crew was Misenus, a trumpeter. Misenus was completely full of himself. In fact, his ego was so big that he decided to challenge the **tempestuous** Triton to a contest to see who was the better trumpeter. (Triton was a master of the conch-shell trumpet. He used it to calm the raging sea, to intimidate **mortals** on land, and to **herald** the arrival of his father, Poseidon.) So what did Triton do? He freed Aeneas's ships, but not before drowning the foolish Misenus.

REALITY CHECK

Aeneas is the hero of Virgil's *Aeneid*, one of the greatest works of ancient Roman literature. This 12-book epic poem traces Aeneas's journey as he flees Troy and settles in Italy.

Want to know more? Go to:
http://classics.mit.edu/Virgil/aeneid.html

Triton blows his own horn!

TRITON'S TRITONS

They're chips off the old block.

Sometimes Triton and Poseidon weren't alone as they traveled through the sea. They were often accompanied by sea creatures that looked just like Triton. The prince of the sea even gave his name to them: tritons. Although these little tritons were smaller, they were otherwise mirror images of the big guy himself, with fish tails and conch-shell trumpets.

REALITY CHECK

The largest conch shell in the world is called Triton's Trumpet. Some of these shells can be up to 20 inches long! This kind of conch shell is found in the western Pacific Ocean.

▼ Profile of Typhon

Sounds Like: tie'-fone

Aliases: God of Storm Winds
Volcano Demon

Generation: ☐ Titan
☐ Olympian
☑ Other: Monster

Special Abilities: Breathing fire
Oozing venom
Throwing mountains

Characteristics: 101 heads
Astonishing height
Serpent legs

Top 10 Things to Know About Me:

10. With my 101 heads, serpent legs, and amazing height, one look at me and you'll run for your life.

9. Venom oozes from my eyes and fire erupts from my mouth.

8. My favorite hobby? Hurling mountains.

7. When I say my kids are monsters, I really mean it!

6. Wonder where I'm hiding out today? Check under Mount Etna in Sicily.

5. I tried to steal Zeus's crown and wife. Unfortunately for me, I lost.

4. There's nothing I love more than a destructive hurricane or volcano.

3. My wife is also part serpent.

2. A little fire still burns in my heart for Hera.

1. If you ask me, the Olympians are all scaredy cats!

> No fair! I wanted to rule heaven and earth.

▼ Family, Flings, Friends, and Foes

▼ Parents	▼ Siblings							▼ Offspring
Tartarus and Gaea	The Titans	The Cyclopes	The Hecatoncheires	The Furies	The Gigantes	Python	Echidna	The Nemean Lion

TYPHON
MONSTER AMBITIONS

Friends, if you're like me, you're burning with rage that an Olympian insider like Zeus is in charge. He can't say he's the biggest creature on Earth! He can't breathe fire! He can't drip venom from his eyes! But *I* can! If you vote for me, I pledge to use all 101 of my heads in service to my—er, our—cause. No god, mortal, or mountain will stand in my way. I'm gonna kill … at the polls!

REALITY CHECK

In mythology, Echidna is Typhon's mate. In reality, echidna is the name of a spiny animal found in Australia and New Guinea. One of the most interesting things about the echidna is that it lays eggs—one of only two mammals to do so; the other is the duck-billed platypus.

Want to know more? Go to: http://www.sandiegozoo. org/animalbytes/t-echidna. html

				▼ Flings		▼ Foes
Cerberus	The Chimera	Hydra	The Sphinx	Echidna	Hera	Zeus

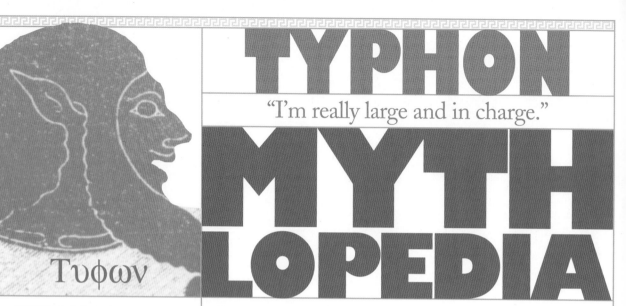

TYPHON

"I'm really large and in charge."

MYTHLOPEDIA

Τυφων

HERE'S LOOKING AT YOU

Why did Typhon strike terror in the hearts and minds of gods and **mortals**? For starters he had 101 heads (1 coming out of his neck and 50 coming out of each hand). Then there was his towering height—his head reached the clouds. But that's not all. Typhon's legs were two hissing serpents, and **venom** oozed out of his eyes.

"My mom was always there for me."

THE BIRTH OF TYPHON

Gaea gives birth to a real monster.

Following the Titanomachy, the epic battle between the Olympians and the Titans, Zeus and the Olympians emerged as the winners. After shoving the Titans into Tartarus, the deepest, darkest part of the **Underworld**, the Olympians battled the Gigantes and defeated them.

This was the last straw for Gaea, the earth goddess and mother of both the Titans and the Gigantes. In her anger she mated with Tartarus and gave birth to the most hideous monster of them all—Typhon. Typhon was so powerful he made the gods look weak and so huge he made the Gigantes look as small as field mice.

Typhon

Zeus

mountain

Typhon

TYPHON VS. ZEUS

Zeus battles Typhon and the big guy wins. But which one?

The only thing bigger than Typhon was his ego. He was so in love with himself that he thought he, not Zeus, should rule the world. After the Gigantes had been defeated by the Olympians, Typhon burst onto the scene and challenged Zeus's throne. The other Olympians took one look at Typhon and fled. Zeus, the only one left to take on the beast, tried to keep Typhon at bay. He threw thunderbolt after thunderbolt at the hideous monster until finally the great Zeus became

exhausted. That's when Typhon made his move. The beast cut out Zeus's **tendons**, leaving the god weak and helpless, and made his way to Mount Olympus. Hermes and Pan spotted the injured Zeus and dashed to his rescue. They retrieved the tendons and patched Zeus back up. Zeus was ready for the next round with Typhon—and this time, he was prepared. As Typhon hurled a mountain at Zeus, the mighty god met it with a huge thunderbolt, forcing the mountain back at Typhon. It landed right on top of the monster, putting an end to his royal ambitions!

LOVE IS BLIND

It's not a match made in heaven …

When Typhon needed a mate, he found Echidna, who perhaps wasn't quite as scary as her man, but she wasn't exactly a beauty queen, either! From the waist up, this she-monster looked like a beautiful sea **nymph**. The problem was from the waist down: Her lower half was a gigantic serpent. Together, Typhon and Echidna produced five terrifying children: the Chimera, Cerberus, the Nemean Lion, the Sphinx, and Hydra!

REALITY CHECK

Legend has it that Typhon was buried alive under Mount Etna in Sicily. Mount Etna is the biggest active volcano in Europe. It stands over eleven thousand feet high and has been erupting lava for more than eight thousand years!

Want to know more? Go to:
http://www.bestofsicily.com/etna.htm

Mount Etna

FAMILY PORTRAIT

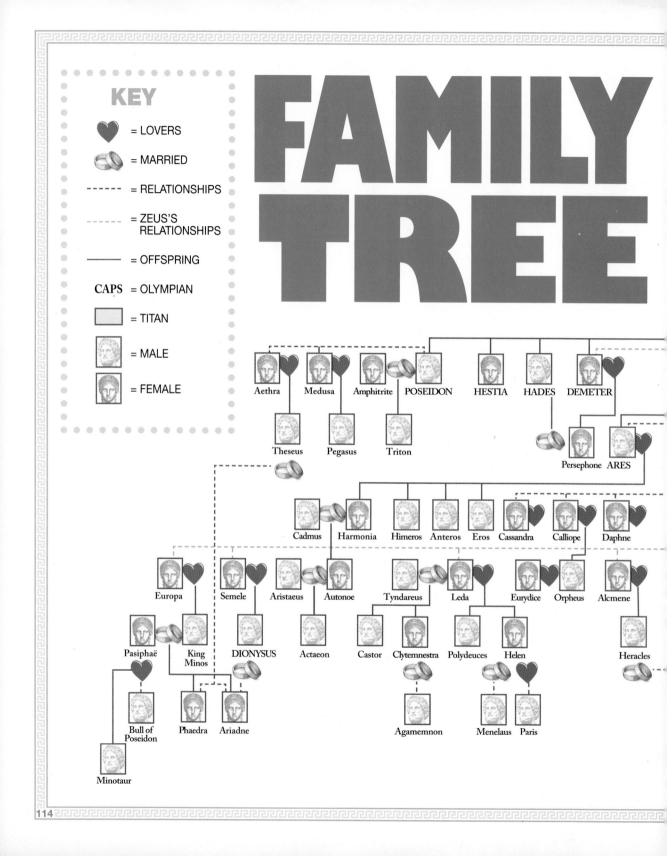

FAMILY TREE

KEY

♥ = LOVERS

💍 = MARRIED

----- = RELATIONSHIPS

------ = ZEUS'S RELATIONSHIPS

—— = OFFSPRING

CAPS = OLYMPIAN

▢ = TITAN

▢ = MALE

▢ = FEMALE

Aethra · Medusa · Amphitrite · POSEIDON · HESTIA · HADES · DEMETER

Theseus · Pegasus · Triton

Persephone · ARES

Cadmus · Harmonia · Himeros · Anteros · Eros · Cassandra · Calliope · Daphne

Europa · Semele · Aristaeus · Autonoe · Tyndareus · Leda · Eurydice · Orpheus · Alcmene

Pasiphaë · King Minos · DIONYSUS · Actaeon · Castor · Clytemnestra · Polydeuces · Helen · Heracles

Bull of Poseidon · Phaedra · Ariadne · Agamemnon · Menelaus · Paris

Minotaur

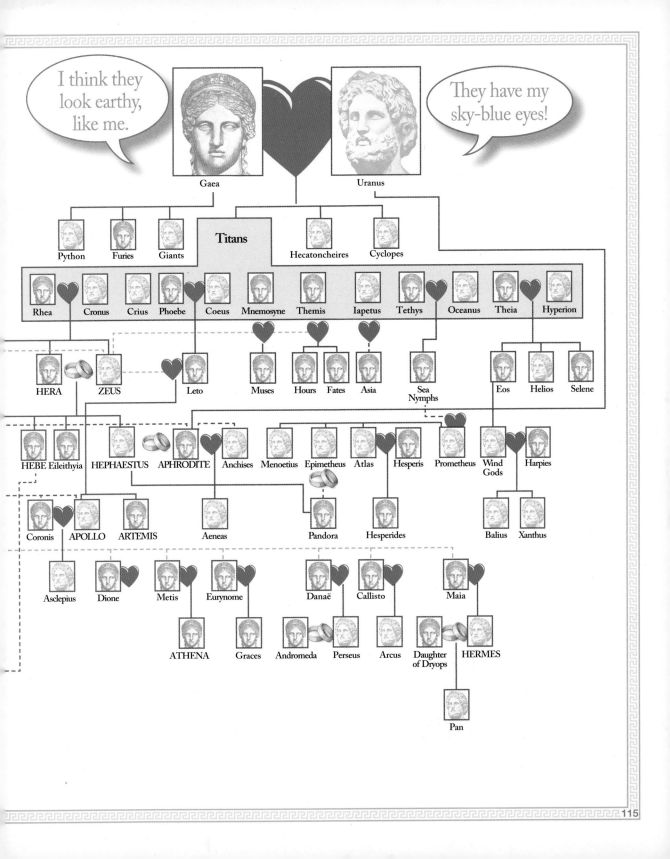

GLOSSARY

arduous   very difficult

Argonauts   the crew that traveled with the hero Jason onboard the ship the *Argo*

barbaric   crude and savage

blacksmiths   workers who shape metal into useful objects

bridle   headgear used to control a horse

chariot   a two-wheeled vehicle drawn by horses

commemorated   honored the memory of a person or event

distraught   very agitated or upset

exiled   forced to leave one's country and live elsewhere

Golden Fleece   the fleece of a golden ram that was the object of the Argonauts' quest

herald   to announce something yet to come

immortal   living forever

invincible   incapable of being conquered

lair   the den of a wild beast

lyre   a U-shaped stringed instrument related to the harp

mayhem   intentional damage or violence

memento   a souvenir or keepsake

mortal   a human being

nymph   a female spirit associated with nature

obstacle   something that gets in the way of progress

oracle	a priestess or priest who communicated the response of a god to a questioner.
penance	an act done to show regret or sorrow
personification	giving human qualities to nonhuman objects or ideas
prophecy	a prediction of a future event
putrid	rotten or foul
pyre	a woodpile used for burning a body as part of a funeral rite
ravaged	devastated, destroyed
rogue	dangerous or corrupt
sickle	a cutting tool with a short handle and a curved metal blade
severed	removed by cutting off or breaking apart
skirmish	a small battle
tempestuous	stormy; intense
tendons	bands of tissue that connect muscles to bones
trident	a spear with three prongs
turban	a headdress formed by cloth wrapped around the head
Underworld	in mythology, the world of the dead, ruled by the god Hades
venom	poisonous material secreted by animals such as snakes and bees, usually through a sting or bite
vial	a small container that can be closed, used to hold liquids
wily	devious or sly

PEGASUS
Zeus placed the winged horse among the stars. Only the front half of his body is shown.

ANDROMEDA
Andromeda was chained to a rock in the sea, threatened by a sea monster, and rescued by the hero Perseus.

CYGNUS
Cygnus the Swan is also known as the Northern Cross. Some mythographers claim the swan is Zeus in disguise.

LYRA
The lyre of the great musician Orpheus was placed among the stars by the Muses.

PERSEUS
The hero slayed the monster Medusa and rescued Andromeda from Cetus, a sea monster. He is shown holding Medusa's head.

HERACLES
Shown kneeling, holding a club, the great hero Heracles was turned into a constellation by Zeus.

Northern Hemisphere

URSA MAJOR
(Great Bear)
Callisto was turned into a bear and shot by Artemis. Zeus placed her among the stars, where she keeps an eye out for Orion, the hunter.

LEO
(Nemean Lion)
The lion of Nemea was slain by the hero Heracles as one of his twelve labors.

ORION

The famed hunter Orion boasted that he would kill every animal on Earth, so Gaea sent a scorpion to sting him. Zeus placed the hunter among the stars and the scorpion nearby *(continues from the Northern Hemisphere to the Southern Hemisphere)*.

CETUS

This sea monster was sent by Poseidon to punish Cassiopeia, the mother of Andromeda, for her vanity.

STARS OF GREEK MYTHOLOGY

Many constellations were named for characters in classical mythology. The practice of taking a being or an object and placing it among the stars is called *catasterism*.

SCORPIO

Sent by Gaea to sting the hunter Orion, the scorpion is placed near him in the sky to remind him of the consequences of boasting.

Southern Hemisphere

CENTAURUS

Centaurus represents the wise Centaur Chiron. Its brightest star, Alpha Centauri, is the closest star to the sun.

ARGO

The ancient constellation Argo Navis, named for the ship that carried Jason and the Argonauts, is made up of three smaller constellations: Puppis (the stern), Carina (the keel), and Vela (the sails).

HYDRA

The serpent was killed by Heracles as another of his twelve labors. In the sky, Hydra is the largest of the 88 constellations *(continues from the Northern Hemisphere to the Southern Hemisphere)*.

Note: Constellations in this illustration may not be exactly where they appear in the sky. For more accurate charts, go to: www.astronomy.com

FURTHER READING

Bolton, Lesley. *The Everything Classical Mythology Book*. Avon, MA: Adams Media, 2002.

Bulfinch, Thomas. *Bulfinch's Greek and Roman Mythology: The Age of Fable*. Mineola, NY: Dover Publications, 2000.

D'Aulaire, Ingri, and Edgar Parin D'Aulaire. *D'Aulaire's Book of Greek Myths*. New York: Random House, Delacorte Press, 1992.

Fleischman, Paul. *Dateline: Troy*. Cambridge, MA: Candlewick Press, 2006.

Hansen, William. *Classical Mythology: A Guide to the Mythical World of the Greeks and Romans*. New York: Oxford University Press, 2005.

Homer. *The Iliad*. Edited by E.V. Rieu. New York: Penguin Classics, 2003.

———. *The Odyssey*. Edited by Bernard Knox. New York: Penguin Classics, 2006.

Osborn, Kevin, and Dana L. Burgess. *The Complete Idiot's Guide to Classical Mythology*. 2nd ed. New York: Penguin, Alpha Books, 2004.

Roberts, Jennifer T., and Tracy Barrett. *The Ancient Greek World*. New York: Oxford University Press, 2004.

Sutcliff, Rosemary. *The Wanderings of Odysseus: The Story of the Odyssey*. New York: Random House, Laurel Leaf, 2005.

———. *Black Ships Before Troy*. London: Frances Lincoln, 2008.

WEB SITES

Encyclopedia Mythica: *http://pantheon.org/*
An online encyclopedia of mythology, folklore, and religion

Greek Mythology: *http://www.greekmythology.com/*
Contains information on gods, goddesses, beasts, and heroes as well as full text of selected books on Greek mythology and literature

Kidipede: Greek Myths: *http://www.historyforkids.org/learn/greeks/religion/greekrelig.htm*
Greek mythology pages of an online encyclopedia of history and science for middle-school students

Mythweb: *http://www.mythweb.com/*
An overview of the Olympians and selected heroes; includes teaching tips

Theoi Greek Mythology: *http://theoi.com/*
Profiles of the Greek gods and goddesses, and other characters from Greek mythology with an emphasis on their appearances in art and literature

INDEX

A

Acheron, River, 33
Achilles, 18, 19
  Balius and Xanthus, 23
  Chiron, 27
Achilles' heel, 23
Achilles tendon, 23
Aegeus, 73, 74
Aello, 52
Aeneas, 107
Aeneid, 107
Agamemnon, 23
Alcyoneus, 49
Amazon rain forest, 17
Amazons, **16–19,** 74
Andromeda, 66
Andromeda (constellation), 118
Anteia, 36
Antiope, 18, 19
Aphrodite, 74
Apollo
  Chiron, 27
  Cyclopes, 41
  Gigantes, 49
  Hercules, 18
  Marsyas, 93
  Oedipus, 101
  oracle, 83
  Python, 88, 89
Arges, 40, 57
Argo, 106
Argo (constellation), 119
Argonauts
  Boreades, 79
  Phineus, 52, 83
  Sirens, 97

Triton, 106
Ariadne, 73, 74
Aristaeus, 49
Artemis, 27, 49
artistic contests, 89
Asclepius, 27, 41
Athena
  Asclepius, 41
  Bellerophon, 37, 79
  Chimera, 36
  Gigantes, 49
  Medusa, 64, 65, 66
  Odysseus, 42
Athens, 19, 73, 74
athletic contests, 89
Atlas, 66

B

Balius, **20–23,** 53
Basilisk, 42
Bellerophon, 36, 37
  Amazons, 18
  Pegasus, 79
blacksmithing, 40, 41, 42
B.O.B. (Benzoate Ostylezene
    Bicarbonate), 42
Boreades, 52, 79, 83
Briareus, 57
bridle, magical, 79
Brontes, 40, 57
bulls, 72

C

Calchas, 82
Caravaggio, 64
Celaeno, 52
Centaur Rocket, 25

Centaurs, **24–29,** 61
Centaurus, 26
Centaurus (constellation), 28,
    119
centipedes, 55
Cerberus, **30–33,** 60, 111
Cerberus (asteroid), 31
Ceto, 67
Cetus (constellation), 119
Charon, 33
Charybdis, 67
Chimera, **34–37**
  Hydra, 60
  Pegasus, 79
  Typhon, 111
Chimera of Arezzo, 35
Chiron, 27, 28
  Asclepius, 41
  Heracles, 61
Chrysaor, 65
Circe, 67
classical mythology, 11
Cocytus, River, 33
conch-shell trumpet, 106, 107
conch shells (sea animals), 107
constellations, 118–119
Cottus, 57
Creon, 100, 101
Crete, 72
Cronus, 27
  Cyclopes, 40
  Gigantes, 48
  Hecatoncheires, 56, 57
curses from the gods, 83
Cyclopean works, 40

Cyclopes, **38–45,** 57
Cyclops, 93
Cygnus (constellation), 118

D
Daedalus, 73, 75
death
   Asclepius, 41
   Harpies, 52, 53
   Underworld, 32, 33
Deianeira, 29, 61
Deino, 67
Delphi, 83, 89
Delphic Games, 89
demons of death, 52, 53
dinosaurs, 37
Dionysus, 18, 74, 92, 93
Doberman Pinschers, 32
dragons, 37
dung beetles, 49

E
earthquakes, 56, 57
Echidna, 60, 111
echidnas (animals), 109
Electra (sea nymph), 52
Elysian Fields, 33
Enyo, 67
Etna, Mount, 42, 111
Euripides, 93
Euryale, 64
Eurydice, 33
Eurystheus, 18 , 29, 32, 61
evil, deflection of, 67
eye patches, 40

F
family tree of the gods, 114–115
fly (insect), 37, 79
flight, human, 75
floods, 88
flying horses, 76–79
forges of Cyclopes, 42
fossils, 37
Furies, 23, 48
future, prediction of, 82, *see also* prophecies

G
Gaea
   Cyclopes, 40
   Gigantes, 48, 49
   Hecatoncheires, 56
   Python, 88
   Typhon, 110
Garden Maze, 73
giants, 48
gifts from the gods, 83
Gigantes, **46–49**
Glaucus, 67
glossary, 116–117
gold belt of Hippolyte, 18
golden apples, 67
Golden Fleece, 106
golden touch, 92
Gorgon blood, 41
Gorgons, 64, 65, 67
Graeae, 67
Great Sphinx at Giza, 99
Great Square of Pegasus (stars), 79
guard dogs, 32

Gulliver's Travels, 48
Gyges, 57

H
Hades, 33
   Cerberus, 32
   helmet of invisibility, 41, 57
   Theseus, 74
Harpies, **50–53,** 79, 83
harpy eagles, 50
Harry Potter series, 26, 33
head of Medusa, 66
Hecate, 49
Hecatoncheires, 40, **54–57**
Hector, 23
Helicon, Mount, 78
helmet of invisibility, 41, 57
Hephaestus, 42, 49
Hera
   Balius and Xanthus, 23
   Centaurs, 26
   Heracles, 18, 29
   Python, 88
   Tiresias, 83
Heracles, 29
   Amazons, 18
   Cerberus, 32
   Chiron, 27, 28
   Gigantes, 49
   Hydra, 61
   Ladon, 67
Heracles (constellation), 29, 118
Hermes, 111
Hesiod, 12
Hesperides, 67
Hippocrene fountain, 78
Hippodamia, 27

Hippolyte, 18
Hippolytus, 18, 19
Homer, 12, 96
Hounds of Zeus, 52
Hydra, **58–61,** 111
Hydra (constellation), 59, 61,
   119
Hydra (freshwater animal), 61
Hydra (Greek island), 61
Hydra (in Marvel comics), 60
Hydra's blood, 28, 29, 61

I
Icarus, 75
Iliad, 12, 22
Iobates, 36, 37
Ixion, 26

J
"Jack and the Beanstalk," 48
Jason
   Boreades, 79
   Chiron, 27
   Phineus, 52, 83
   Sirens, 97
   Triton, 106
jellyfish, 63
Jocasta, 101
judges of the dead, 33

K
Kang, 42
Kodos, 42

L
labors of Hercules, 29
   Amazons, 18
   Cerberus, 32

golden apples, 67
   Hydra, 61
labyrinths *see* mazes
Ladon, 67
Laius, 101
Lapiths, 26, 27
Leo (constellation), 118
Lethe, River, 33
Leto, 88
Little Mermaid, 106
logos based on myths, 77, 97
Lorelei, 97
Lycia, 36
Lyra (constellation), 118

M
Marsyas, 93
mazes, 72, 73, 75
Meadows of Asphodel, 33
Medusa, **62–69,** 78
medusae (marine animals), 63
Medusa's Head (stars), 65
Megara, 29
mermen, 106, 107
Michael "Mike" Wazowski, 42
Midas, 92, 93
Minos, 19, 72, 75
Minotaur, **70–75**
Misenus, 107
Mopus, 82
Mr. Ed, 21
Muses, 78
music
   Apollo and Marsyas, 93
   Orpheus, 33
   Sirens, 96
   Triton and Misenus, 107

myths
   defined, 11
   purpose, 12

N
Naxos, 74
Nemean Lion, 60, 111
Nephele, 26
Neptune (planet), 105
Nessus, 29
New York Giants, 47
Nicothoe, 52
Norse mythology, 48
nymphs, 48

O
Ocypete, 52
Odysseus
   Calchas, 82
   Cyclopes, 42, 43
   Sirens, 96
Odyssey, 12, 96
Oedipus, 100, 101
Olympians, 40
   Gigantes, 49
   Hecatoncheires, 56, 57
   monsters, 110
Olympic Games, 89
Olympus, Mount, 49, 79, 111
one-eyed beasts, 42
Ophiuchus (constellation), 41
Oracle at Delphi, 83, 89, 101,
   see also Pythia
Oracles and Prophets *see*
   Prophets and Oracles
Orion (constellation), 119
Orpheus, 33, 97

P

Pactolus River, 92
Pan, 111
parasailing, 75
Parnassus, Mount, 81, 83, 88
Pasiphaë, 72
Patroclus, 23
Pegasus, 18, 37, **76–79**
  Chimera, 36
  Medusa, 65
Pegasus (constellation), 79, 118
Peleus, 22
Penthesileia, 18, 19
Periboea., 101
Persephone, 33, 74
Perseus
  Graeae, 67
  helmet of invisibility, 41
  Medusa, 65, 66
Perseus (constellation), 65, 118
Persis, 67
Phaedra, 19
Philonoe, 37
Philyra, 27
Phineus, 52, 79, 83
Phlegethon, River, 33
Phorcys, 67
Picasso, Pablo, 71
Pirithous, 27
Pleakley, Agent Wendy, 42
Podarge, 22, 52, 53
poisons
  Circe, 67
  Hydra, 28, 29, 61
  Typhon, 60, 110
Polybus, 101

Polyphemus, 42, 43
Poseidon
  Balius and Xanthus, 22
  Cyclopes, 42
  Medusa, 64, 65
  Minotaur, 72
  trident, 41, 57
  Triton, 107
Prometheus, 28
prophecies
  Achilles, 22, 23
  Oedipus, 101
Prophets and Oracles, **80–85**
Proteus, 36
Pythia, 83, 89, *see also* Oracle
  at Delphi
Pythian, 89
Pythian Games, 89
Pytho, 89, *see also* Delphi
Python, 83, **86–89**
pythons, 87

R

Rhea, 40
Rhine River, 97
riddle of the Sphinx, 100
Roman deities, 11

S

Sagittarius (constellation), 28
salamanders, 95
satyr butterflies, 91
satyr plays, 93
Satyrs, **90–93**
Scorpio (constellation), 119
Scylla, 67
sea monsters, 66, 67

Serpent Bearer (constellation),
  41
serpents
  Echidna, 111
  Hydra, 60
  Medusa, 64
  Python, 83
  Typhon, 110
shield of Athena, 65, 66
Silenus, 92
"Siren Song," 97
Sirens, 33, **94–97**
snakes *see* serpents
Snatchers, 52
songs of Sirens, 96
Sphinx, **98–103**
  Hydra, 60
  Typhon, 111
Starbucks logo, 97
Steropes, 40, 57
Stheno, 64
stone, turn to, 65
stone walls, 40
storms, 52
Styx, River, 23, 33

T

talking horses, 21, 23, 53
Tartarus, 33
  Cyclopes, 40
  Hecatoncheires, 56, 57
  Typhon, 110
temple of Apollo, 81, 89, 101
Thaumas, 52
Thebes, 100, 101

Theogony, 12
Theseus
  Amazons, 18, 19
  Chiron, 27
  Minotaur, 73, 74
Thetis, 22
thunderbolts, 41, 57
Tiresias, 83, 101
Titanomachy, 110
Titans, 40, 57, 110
tomb figures, 53
touch, golden, 92
tridents, 41, 57, 106
Triton, **104–107**
Triton (moon of Neptune), 105
Tritonis, Lake, 106
tritons (sea animals), 107
Triton's Trumpet (seashell), 107
Trojan Horse, 82
Trojan War
  Amazons, 18, 19
  Balius and Xanthus, 23
  Calchas, 82
  Odysseus, 42
trumpet contest, 107
Turanga Leela, 42
twelve labors of Hercules *see*
    labors of Hercules
Typhon, 61, **108–111**

U
Underworld, 32, 33
Uranus
  Cyclopes, 40
  Gigantes, 48
  Hecatoncheires, 56, 57
Ursa Major (constellation), 118

V
venom, 60, 110
Virgil, 107
volcanoes, 57
  Cyclopes, 42
  Hecatoncheires, 56
  Typhon, 111
vultures, 52

W
walls of stone, 40
weapons, 41, 57
west wind, 22, 53
whirlpools, 67
winds, 52, 53
winged heroes, 79
women warriors, 18
Wonder Woman, 17, 19
wood nymphs (butterflies), 91
wooden horse, 82

X
X-Men, 39
Xanthus, **20–23,** 53

Z
Zephyrus, 22, 53
Zeus
  Asclepius, 41
  Bellerophon, 37, 79
  Centaurs, 26
  Chiron, 27, 61
  Harpies, 52, 53
  Hecatoncheires, 57
  Phineus, 52, 83
  thunderbolts, 57
  Tiresias, 83
  Titans, 40
  Typhon, 111

Marie O'Neill, Creative Director
Cheryl Clark, Editor in Chief
Caroline Anderson, Director of Photography
Cian O'Day, Ed Kasche, Jay Pastorello, Photo Research
SimonSays Design!, Book Production and Design

Illustrations:
Paul Meisel: cover, 4–5, 7, 23, 43, 68–69, 78, 84–85, 112–113, 118–119, 121
G.F. Newland: 102–103
Rupert Van Wyk (Beehive Illustration): 44-45, 110
XNR Productions, Inc.: 118–119